WHO'S RUNNING YOUR LIFE?

OTHER BOOKS BY JULES ARCHER

African Firebrand: Kenyatta of Kenya
Angry Abolitionist: William Lloyd Garrison
Battlefield President: Dwight D. Eisenhower
China in the Twentieth Century
Chou En-lai
Colossus of Europe: Metternich
Congo
The Dictators
Epidemic!
The Executive "Success"
The Extremists: Gadflies of American Society
Famous Young Rebels
Fighting Journalist: Horace Greeley
From Whales to Dinosaurs
Front-Line General: Douglas MacArthur
Hawks, Doves, and the Eagle
Ho Chi Minh: The Legend of Hanoi
Hunger on Planet Earth
Indian Foe, Indian Friend
Laws That Changed America
Legacy of the Desert
Man of Steel: Joseph Stalin
Mao Tse-tung: A Biography
Mexico and the United States
1968: Year of Crisis
The Philippines' Fight for Freedom
The Plot to Seize the White House
Police State
Red Rebel: Tito of Yugoslavia
Resistance
Revolution in Our Time
Riot! A History of Mob Action in the United States
The Russians and the Americans
Strikes, Bombs, and Bullets: Big Bill Haywood and the I.W.W.
Superspies
They Made a Revolution: 1776
Thorn in Our Flesh: Castro's Cuba
Treason in America: Disloyalty Versus Dissent
Trotsky: World Revolutionary
Twentieth-Century Caesar: Benito Mussolini
Uneasy Friendship: France and the United States
The Unpopular Ones
Washington vs. Main Street
Watergate: America in Crisis
World Citizen: Woodrow Wilson
You and the Law

WHO'S RUNNING YOUR LIFE?

A Look at Young People's Rights

Jules Archer

Illustrated with photographs

HARCOURT BRACE JOVANOVICH
NEW YORK AND LONDON
ROSLINDALE

Copyright © 1979 by Jules Archer

All rights reserved. No part
of this publication may be reproduced or
transmitted in any form or by any means,
electronic or mechanical, including photocopy,
recording, or any information storage and
retrieval system, without permission
in writing from the publisher.

Requests for permission to make copies
of any part of the work should be mailed to:
Permissions, Harcourt Brace Jovanovich, Inc.,
757 Third Avenue,
New York, New York 10017

The author and publisher wish to thank Holt, Rinehart and Winston, Publishers, for permission to reprint the poem "The Golf Links Lie So Near the Mill" from *Portraits and Protests* by Sarah N. Cleghorn. All rights reserved; and the McGraw-Hill Book Company for permission to cite certain research studies from the book *A Child's Journey* by Julius Segal and Herbert Yahraes. Copyright © 1978 by Julius Segal and Herbert Yahraes.

Printed in the United States of America

Library of Congress Cataloging in Publication Data

Archer, Jules.
Who's running your life?

Bibliography: p.
Includes index.
SUMMARY: Discusses the rights of children and young adults, including those concerning family life, school, working, and personal freedom.
1. Children's rights—Juvenile literature.
2. Children's rights—United States—Juvenile literature.
[1. Children's rights.   2. Law]   I. Title.
HV713.A7   362.7   78-20566
ISBN 0-15-296058-9

First edition

B C D E

Affectionately for my daughter by marriage
MAUREEN ARCHER

CONTENTS

ACKNOWLEDGMENTS ix
WHO'S RUNNING YOUR LIFE? 3
YOUR BIRTHRIGHTS 11
YOUR RIGHT TO PROTECTION FROM HARM 21
YOUR FAMILY RIGHTS AS A CHILD 31
YOUR RIGHTS IN PRIMARY SCHOOL 43
YOUR FAMILY RIGHTS AS A TEEN-AGER 55
YOUR RIGHTS IN JUNIOR HIGH AND HIGH SCHOOL 71
YOUR RIGHT TO LOOK AS YOU PLEASE 85

CONTENTS

YOUR RIGHT TO READ, SEE, AND HEAR WHAT YOU LIKE 91

YOUR RIGHT TO LOVE AND BE LOVED 103

YOUR RIGHT TO WORK OR NOT TO WORK 117

YOUR RIGHT TO PROTEST AGAINST AUTHORITY 127

YOUR RIGHT TO JUSTICE UNDER THE LAW 135

YOUR RIGHTS TOMORROW 149

BIBLIOGRAPHY AND RECOMMENDED READING 157

INDEX 163

ACKNOWLEDGMENTS

For their invaluable help, I am greatly indebted to Harvey F. Batton, librarian, International Labour Organization, Liaison Office with the United Nations; Janice Fuhrmann, reporter, Watsonville (California) *Register-Pajaronian*; Melinda Greenblatt, assistant director, and Anne Pellowski, director, Information Center on Children's Cultures, International Year of the Child Resource Center, United States Committee for UNICEF; James L. Perine, assistant to the dean for university park programs, College of Human Development, Pennsylvania State University; and especially to Dr. Julius Segal and Herbert Yahraes of the National Institute of Mental Health for permission to cite certain research studies from their book, *A Child's Journey* (McGraw-Hill, 1978).

I am also grateful for the generous help of the following people, whom I interviewed in Santa Cruz, California, and who provided me with a wealth of material and case histories: Joe Blackman, assistant superintendent in charge of secondary education,

ACKNOWLEDGMENTS

Santa Cruz School District; Patrick Graham, psychiatric technician, Child and Family Counseling Center of Santa Cruz County; Terry Moriarty and Margaret Newport of Youth Services; Alice Enna, school program coordinator and third grade teacher; Robert M. Patterson, assistant district attorney in charge of juvenile crime, Santa Cruz County; Janet Reed, Liz DiCristoforo, and Maria Bacci of Children's Protective Services; and Mary Zuccaro, community educator in charge of school programs and special counselor for teens and parents, Planned Parenthood.

And in Santa Clara County, California, Hank Giarretto, director, Child Sexual Abuse Treatment Program.

JULES ARCHER

WHO'S RUNNING YOUR LIFE?

WHO'S RUNNING YOUR LIFE?

You're a senior at Douglas MacArthur High School in Levittown, New York, and you're mad as blazes. Here it is eight weeks after school was supposed to start, and you haven't attended a single class yet. Not because you haven't wanted to, but because all your teachers are out on strike to protest an eighteen-month wage freeze and impending layoffs by the school board. And neither side will compromise.

Meanwhile, you've lost two valuable months of education—highly important months because they will affect your chances of winning a college acceptance in March.

Along with sixty-nine other angry students, you decide to stage a sit-in protest in your school to dramatize your outrage at the adults who are running your school life and doing a miserable job of it. On October 22, 1978, you invade the office of Principal Robert Simko, spending the night there and in the hallway, occupying yourselves with games, talk, and reading.

Reporters from the New York *Post* invade the school to shoot photos and conduct interviews. Mark Goldberg, president of SACRIFICE (Student Action Committee Regarding Interests for Children's Education), declares, "We are trying to say that kids care and want to go back to school." The sit-in ends the next day, after one furious sixteen-year-old boy punches out a windowpane in the principal's office. "If anyone is hurt, it defeats our purpose," Goldberg explains. But the sit-in has made its point.

The next day, student sit-ins spread to two more Levittown schools. About seventy-five students sit down outside the office of Principal John Sullivan at Division Avenue Senior High School and another fifty at the junior high school nearby. Sullivan agrees to meet with General Student Organization president Terry Schoenig.

"We're the victims and no one cares," she complains.

Sullivan says of the demonstrators, "They're good kids."

The following day, 250 students stage a march and rally chanting, "We want school!", and carrying banners that read: "We Want Our Teachers Back in School." That evening, a hundred students march to the homes of three school board members to protest, while other students express bitterness to teachers on picket lines in front of the schools.

The outrage of students and their parents convinces school authorities that they had better do something quickly about the lack of classes for 10,000 children in the school districts. On the following day, administrative and substitute personnel are rushed into classrooms, and 4,000 students, determined to miss no more schooling, attend while the strike goes on.

You and the other students don't know whether to blame the teachers or the school board. But senior class president Lynn Leopold speaks for all of you when she declares, "We're the ones who are hurt. They don't care about us and we're sick of it."

The students staged the sit-ins, senior Craig Hurwitz explains, "because somebody had to do something!"

* * *

WHO'S RUNNING YOUR LIFE?

As a young person, you have the power to affect those around you through your words and actions. By giving rein to your natural curiosity, intelligence, and creativity, you can exercise your rights responsibly, and your political power will grow as you do.

It's understandable if you feel impatient to become an adult and take control of your own life. When you are allowed to exercise those rights that are yours today, you learn how to act as a responsible citizen tomorrow. You will not become one of those unthinking adults who allow the government or their employer to run their lives for them. As for now, being relatively powerless is not the most enjoyable of conditions, but it is the condition under which you are forced to live as long as you are a legal "minor."

It would be incredible to think of Congress today passing a bill to deprive the citizens of thirty-six states of the right to run their own lives.

Yet an equal number of American citizens—almost 70 million—are now compelled to live under laws that entitle other Americans to make all their decisions for them. Only one difference sets them apart from those who control them: they are eighteen years of age or younger.

Many children were, and still are, cruelly abused, neglected, or exploited by their society, or by parents made desperate by poverty or other problems. Even when well-meaning governments have passed laws designed to protect and nurture them, children themselves have rarely been consulted about their own needs and aspirations.

Thomas Jefferson thought it wrong that the older generation should have the right of absolute control over the younger generation. Each generation, he suggested in a letter written in 1813, should consider itself "a distinct nation, with a right, by the will of its majority, to bind themselves, but none to bind the succeeding generation, any more than they have the right to bind the inhabitants of another country."

At the dawn of the twentieth century, a Swedish essayist hopefully predicted that it would be the "Century of the Child." The nations of the world did, indeed, begin to pay more attention to the problems of young people than ever before. New laws gave special consideration to their needs and rights.

In 1946, the United Nations created UNICEF, the international children's fund. It provided aid to some 57 million young people in over a hundred countries for health services, family and child welfare, disease control, nutrition, and emergency relief.

Yet even UNICEF gave no representation on its governing councils to any older teen-agers to help decide how, where, and when needy youngsters of the world should be helped.

In running young people's lives, adults have persisted in thinking of them as a uniform group—"the children"—instead of as individuals. Books with titles like *How to Handle Adults* are simply not published, but there has never been a dearth of books that could be called *How to Handle Children*.

It may often seem like an unfair world to you, a world in which adults have total power and frequently use it without regard for or understanding of your feelings. In your darker moments, you may even regard your own parents as enemies, rather than as friends.

You have no choice of the people with whom you must live, or of the schools that your parents and the state decide you must attend, or of the nature of the society in which you must grow up. Yet you are taught that freedom of choice is one of the traditions that make America great. It is understandable, therefore, that as you mature and grow more capable of deciding what is best for you, you feel entitled to a greater voice in decisions affecting your own life. You have a right to ask, "Who's running my life—and to what extent should I have something to say about it?" This book attempts to explore the power situation affecting school-age young people. It analyzes their moral and legal rights, as well as the responsibilities that go with the exercise of those rights. And it suggests ways to go about obtaining them.

We will take a look at the various ways in which adults run your life from birth until the day the law considers you emancipated into adulthood. And we will consider your rights, legal and moral, as a minor.

You have a right to protection from harm. The law looks severely upon parents or guardians who take advantage of a child's relative helplessness and dependency by abusing the child physically or mentally. Adults charged with the care of a child may also lose custody by neglecting the child's needs.

New efforts are being made to spotlight and help such children, especially an estimated 60,000 to 100,000 young people who are sexually abused by family members or friends every year. In 1978, the National Center on Child Abuse and Neglect provided $43,000 to finance an experimental sex-abuse phone hot line operated by Child and Family Services of Knoxville, Tennessee, under a federal grant for children in the area.

Nine hundred calls a month are received. The average caller is a fifteen-year-old girl, although children as young as seven have appealed to the hot line for help. They are connected with counselors, who reassure them and set in motion investigations to rescue the frightened, unhappy victims.

In addition to your right to protection from harm, you have family rights both as a pre-teen and a teen-ager. We hear a great deal today about the "human rights" of adults under governments that oppress them. But we hear little about the human rights of children in our own country who may be suffering under tyrannical, unreasonable, or neurotic parents.

Professor Ulla Jacobssen, a professor of law at Sweden's Stockholm University, has created a world-wide stir in legal circles by a proposal based on her research on the neglected rights of children. She has drafted legislation proposing that young people whose lives are made intolerable at home should have the right to "divorce" their parents.

"A very large number of thirteen- to nineteen-year-olds have serious relationship disturbances with one parent," Professor Jacobssen reports. "In older days it used to be the boy who ran away to sea—or who wanted to. Now it's the girls who often want to leave home, where they can no longer communicate with parents, especially the father."

In Malmö, Sweden's third largest city, many children complain to officials about nagging parents, drunkenness in the family, fights between parents, religious disagreements, and loneliness for an absent divorced parent. When officials determine that teen-agers have serious problems at home and are not just experiencing the normal temporary bout of adolescent rebellion, they permit such young people to leave home and live temporarily in one of a handful of apartments set aside for emergency cases.

You also have certain rights as a student in primary, junior high, and senior high school. What can you do when things go wrong for you in this important area of your life? If you find some of your teachers or many of your courses intolerable, is the only answer dropping out?

Dropping out when you are old enough to get permission may seem, at first, like liberation. But drop-outs often find themselves severely handicapped in the competition for decent jobs. In addition, they feel a psychological stigma of failure that erodes their self-esteem.

In University City, Missouri, one anguished eighteen-year-old high school drop-out returned to his former school with a .38 caliber revolver in 1978 and began a shooting spree that wounded three students, one critically, and a junior high school principal.

In this book we will also consider your right to look as you please and to resist clothing and grooming requirements made upon you by the adult world. We will also discuss your right to read, see, and hear what you like and society's attempts to censor films, TV, books, magazines, and music they feel harmful for you.

Of vital importance to you and every teen-ager is your right to love and be loved. How much of this phase of your life should be controlled by your parents? When do you have a right to demand that the reins be loosened? If you're a girl and you find yourself pregnant, do you have a right to an abortion without your parents' knowledge and consent?

In 1976, the Supreme Court ruled that laws that gave parents "absolute" veto power over a young girl's decision to have an abortion were unconstitutional. But in October 1978, the Court said it would study a new Massachusetts case, to decide whether states may require unwed girls under eighteen to get the consent of parents or a judge before undergoing an abortion.

In the area of employment, you have the right to work, as well as the right to be protected from the exploitation of child labor.

The question of your rights under the Constitution is explored in the chapter on your right to protest against adult authority. Is the protection of the Constitution only for adult Americans or is it meant for you, too?

Society has been moving in the direction of increased rights for groups who have in the past been discriminated against—blacks, other ethnic groups, women, homosexuals, and now, at last, children. Young people who get into trouble are beginning to get legal counsel like that available to adults. The state is being stripped of its power to arrest you for offenses that are not also considered offenses for adults.

At the same time, serious juvenile crimes are no longer being punished lightly. In Endicott, New York, a thirteen-year-old boy was arraigned in October 1978 on the charge of shooting to death a fifteen-year-old boy following an argument. Formerly, he could have been sentenced, as a juvenile, only to a maximum of eighteen months in a reformatory. Under a new state law, he could face an adult murder charge and be sentenced to prison for life.

Finally, this book will consider what your rights are likely to be in the world of tomorrow, in school, at home, and in society. In this era of rapid social change, tomorrow may arrive before you leave childhood behind. If not, the coming changes will certainly affect your younger brothers and sisters and your own future children.

But first let us examine the birthrights that are yours merely as a result of the obligation your parents and society have incurred by permitting you to enter this world.

YOUR BIRTHRIGHTS

At the age of twenty-five, Tom Hansen sued his parents in a Boulder, Colorado, district court. He charged that they had raised him so badly that he would need psychiatric care for the rest of his life. They were accused of willful and wanton neglect of his childhood needs for food, clothing, shelter, and psychological support at crucial periods of his life.

When only fourteen, Hansen's lawyer said, he had been forced to "work long hours at menial labor on little food" and had been suspended from school as a consequence. His father had treated him as a "social outcast, subjecting him to humiliation and ridicule and physically attacking him."

Hansen now asked to be awarded $350,000 in damages.

The case is still pending in court as this book is written. Interestingly, Hansen's parents are fighting it on the basis that since his suit is being brought so long after the alleged neglect and abuse took place, the statute of limitations makes the case invalid.

This unusual case raises provocative questions. What are the birthrights of children—rights to which every child in the world is entitled from parents and from society?

For centuries, children were considered the property of parents, to be used and controlled as their parents saw fit. They lived largely at the mercy of adults—both adults who cared for them and adults who did not. Adults made the rules that governed the child's world. Children who could not comply with those rules were made to suffer for it.

So-called illegitimate children are a case in point. If you had been born to an unmarried mother, you would have been stigmatized as a "bastard" and often treated worse than a leper. Not only would the law discriminate against you, but you would often be shunned by "legitimate" children whose parents did not consider you a "fit" playmate.

You would usually have been denied the right to inherit any property from your father. In ancient Rome, as a newborn child you would be laid at your father's feet. Only if he raised you in his arms, acknowledging by this act that you were his own, would you have been admitted to all the rights and privileges of membership in a Roman family. But if he did not take you up, you became an outcast, with no family. You could then legally be taken from the house by a slave and left by the roadside to perish. You would survive only if someone discovered you, wanted you, and adopted you.

During the Middle Ages, you would have been considered "the child of no one." You would have possessed no legal rights. Most adults would have scorned you as a "product of sin." People who tried to help you would have been accused of condoning immorality and encouraging licentious behavior.

In England, you would have been the responsibility of Poor Law authorities until taxpayers revolted in 1576 against being burdened with the support of illegitimate children. In that year, Parliament passed a Bastardy Act that held that giving such children alms was "defrauding" the elderly poor of aid and "an evil example and encouragement of the lewd life." The law ordered natural parents to pay for the upkeep of their illegitimate children.

Unwanted by the community, a burden to your mother, shunned by your father, you probably would have been abandoned physically. You might have been turned out of your home without even shoes or sufficient clothes. Or perhaps sold to itinerant peddlers.

In the United States, the period from 1880 to 1914 saw the rise of a movement to crusade for children's rights. Jacob Riis, a Danish-born reporter and reformer, tried to improve the conditions for children of immigrants in the slums of New York City in 1892. In 1904, the National Child Labor Committee was organized. Their agitation diminished the exploitation and mishandling of children. In 1912, the United States Children's Bureau was established to "investigate and report on all matters pertaining to welfare of children and child life among all classes of our people."

Growing awareness of children's rights was reflected in President Woodrow Wilson's proclamation of 1919 as Children's Year and the calling of a White House conference on child welfare standards. In 1921, the Sheppard-Towner Act provided infant and maternal community services designed to give all children a good start in life. In 1940, another White House conference deplored the inequality of opportunities available to children from deprived homes. In 1978 the New York State Court of Appeals ruled that you have legal rights even as an *unborn* child. In a unanimous decision, the court held that for the last five months of pregnancy, the unborn child of a welfare recipient is entitled to welfare payments in his or her own right "so that proper prenatal care so vital to physical and mental well-being of the unborn child can be provided."

In 1959, the General Assembly of the United Nations issued a Declaration of the Rights of the Child. "Mankind owes to the child," it said in part, "the best it has to give. . . . The child shall enjoy special protection.... The child shall be entitled from his birth to a name and a nationality.... The child shall have the right to adequate nutrition, housing, recreation, and medical services. The child who is physically, mentally, or socially handicapped shall be given the special treatment, education, and care required by his particular condition....

"The child ... shall, wherever possible, grow up in the care and under the responsibility of his parents, and in any case in an atmosphere of affection and of moral and material security.... Society and the public authorities shall have the duty to extend particular care to children without a family and to those without adequate means of support.... The child is entitled to receive education, which shall be free and compulsory, at least in the elementary stages....

"The child shall be protected against all forms of neglect, cruelty, and exploitation.... The child shall not be admitted to employment before an appropriate minimum age [nor] ... in any occupation ... which would prejudice his health or education.... The child shall be protected from practices which may foster racial, religious, and any other form of discrimination."

But seventeen years later, the UN was forced to admit that its declaration had done little to improve conditions for most of the world's children. On December 21, 1976, the General Assembly passed a resolution setting aside 1979 as the International Year of the Child. The world community was urged to demonstrate its concern for the present and future condition of all youth.

Despite all these efforts, even in the prosperous United States, the UN's basic rights of children are missing from the lives of about 17 million, according to Dr. Julius Segal and Herbert Yahraes of the National Institute of Mental Health. Many suffer from physical and emotional abuse and neglect.

The world picture is no less disturbing. The UN estimates that every night some 230 million children go to bed hungry. Robert McNamara, president of the World Bank, pointed out that as many as one in four children in the underdeveloped nations die before their fifth birthday. They perish from starvation and the malnutrition that makes them susceptible to any of a dozen dangerous diseases.

Fifty years ago, District Judge Leon R. Yankwich declared in a court decision, "There are no illegitimate children—only illegitimate parents," but society continues to abuse the illegitimate child. If you lack a legitimate father, your birth certificate may indicate this fact, stigmatizing you when you are forced to produce the certificate while registering for school, jobs, and the like. You may also be made to feel ashamed of your lack of an "acceptable" family background, dreading that friends and those you care about may find out, causing you humiliation.

A UN study made in 1965 found that, in every nation, death rates for the children of unmarried mothers average 73 percent higher than for the children of married parents. Single mothers are often anxious and sometimes become neurotic or even psychotic, communicating emotional upset to their infants. A Toronto study of illegitimate teen-agers found 47 percent of them "maladjusted." One in five manifested behavior problems that had gotten them into difficulties.

A 1966 study of child abuse reported to the Columbia University School of Public Health that illegitimate children were three and a half times more likely to be maltreated than legitimate children.

Today, about 200,000 unmarried American girls give birth to babies each year. Some 94 percent now decide to keep them rather than give them up for adoption. "Mothers who are obliged to assume double parental responsibility, often working away from home to earn bare livelihoods for themselves and their children, struggle against almost insurmountable difficulties in guiding and training them," reported Emma O. Lundberg and Katharine F. Lenroot in an early study for the United States Children's Bureau.

As an illegitimate child, you could be placed with foster parents who may be less likely than a legitimate child's parents to deal patiently with troublesome conduct. You may even find yourself committed to an institution as "uncontrollable."

With so many handicaps, it is hardly surprising that, as an illegitimate child, you might develop a gloomy outlook on life and strike back at society through delinquent behavior. Lundberg and Lenroot found that your chances of becoming delinquent were double those of legitimate children. But prejudice is partly to blame. You would be given fewer chances and brought to court for less serious offenses than children with two legal parents.

The tragedy of neglected and abused children is that they are helpless victims of the society into which they were born, or of their parents, or both. They have no control over their own lives, no voice in what happens to them, no blame for the misery that overwhelms them.

At present, there are three to five million adopted persons in the United States. Half of them are still children, most born out of wedlock. Many want to know who their natural parents are, but in most cases records are sealed, adoption agencies are sworn to silence, and birth certificates have been legally altered. The purpose of these precautions is to prevent the disruption of the adoption relationship.

But not knowing who your "real" mother and father are, if you're adopted, can become a source of frustration and anxiety, making you feel different from other children. California psychiatrist Arthur D. Sorosky believes that it is important for your mental health to know. Two organizations, Orphan Voyage and Adoptees Liberty Movement Association (ALMA), have sprung up to help adoptees find their natural parents. ALMA is now fighting the legality of sealed records in the courts.

Most authorities today agree that you have a right to be told you are an adopted child as early as possible, preferably with stress on the fact that you were "chosen" to be your adopted parents' child, while other parents had no choice in the matter. You also have a right to learn from your adopted parents the extent of their knowledge about your natural parents—their ages, family background, medical history, education, physical description, interests, other children or relatives. Generally, adopted parents do not know the names of the real parents.

You also have a right to know the name of the adoption agency so that, if you insist, you can pressure the agency to let you locate your real parents. Some agencies will agree to contact your real parents, usually your mother, and see whether she will consent to meet you. In many such cases she is overjoyed by the opportunity and may actually have been trying to trace you as well.

In a far worse plight than illegitimate or adopted children are children born in extremely poor homes. In 1977, Professor Kenneth Keniston noted for the Carnegie Council on Children, "In tar-paper shacks without plumbing in rural Maine there are children who risk freezing to death for lack of heat on subzero winter nights. In Cincinnati slums there are children who have never slept in a bed of their own or seen a doctor."

Estimating that from 25 percent to 33 percent of children suffer from the lack of decent food, shelter, and medicine, Keniston observed that they are hidden away from the view of the majority of Americans on desert reservations, in mountain communities, city slums, tenant farmer shacks, and migrant worker barracks.

If you are one of these children, you probably also suffer from being labeled "dirty, stupid, and worthless—like the parents." Lacking the advantages of children from comfortable homes, you cannot keep up with them academically. Soon you might accept the view of yourself that you are inadequate, bound to fail in life. Then it becomes a self-fulfilling prophecy.

Equally unfair has been the treatment of black children in the United States. In the early days of black slavery in America, if you were an infant born to a slave mother, you were declared a slave even if your father was white.

"Whereas some doubts have arisen," declared an act of the Virginia Assembly in 1662, "whether children got by an Englishman upon a negro woman should be slave or free . . . all children born in this country shall be held bond or free only according to the condition of the mother." Thus you would have found yourself forced to share the servitude of your black mother while your white father lived in freedom and comfort in a big white plantation mansion.

Until 1954, most American blacks were doomed to an inadequate education in an inferior separate school often taught by poorly trained teachers. In that year, however, the U.S. Supreme Court handed down an historic decision. The verdict in *Brown* v. *Board of Education* ruled that "separate but equal" schools for blacks violated their constitutional rights under the Fourteenth Amendment, and that separate schools were inherently unequal.

Local courts then ordered many communities to integrate all schools by busing black students to white schools and white students to black schools. Angry white parents rioted in a number of school districts to prevent busing. Many schools were eventually integrated. In many others, however, black students continued to make up the vast majority of the student body.

As a child of a black or other minority family, you may feel discouraged about your prospects. If you live in a poverty-ridden home in the slums, in many cases you may not be able to get the same kind of support most white children get. Keeping pace can become increasingly difficult. And even when you graduate from high school, job opportunities for you may be scarce.

You may also suffer from racism in a society that wounds your self-esteem and self-confidence. You may feel perpetually haunted by the question, "Why did I have to be born different? Why *me?*" It may vex you that most white people can't see the individual inside the skin, but talk about "you people," as though all blacks, or all Puerto Ricans or Chicanos, are the same.

In 1965, the government sought to help minority preschoolers with a program called Project Head Start, to let them catch up with children from more advantaged homes. The following year, a Child Nutrition Act provided financial aid for new breakfast programs for children in poor areas of the country.

The problems of poor and minority children are, of course, not unique to the United States. In England, many whose parents are on public assistance rolls are underfed and badly clothed. Their fathers are generally absent, sometimes in prison. Their mothers sometimes neglect them while gambling in bingo halls or drinking in pubs.

One British teacher revealed that such children followed her around the school, creeping back into the classroom or cloakroom and huddling in a corner. On nonschool days they wandered about, knocking at doors to see if someone would take them in.

The majority of children born in democracies, nevertheless, enjoy far more of their birthrights than those born under other systems of government. In underdeveloped Third World countries, *most* children grow up poverty-ridden. Many are undernourished and underschooled, have poor health, are put to work at a very early age and given little opportunity to rise out of the cycle of grinding poverty that entrapped their parents.

Children born in communist countries occupy a position halfway between the capitalist democracies and the Third World countries. There is greater equality in the treatment of children. Few are as privileged as middle-class children in the democracies, but almost none live as miserably as the poorest children in the democracies.

Most governments in the world today acknowledge, in theory if not always in fact, the birthrights of every infant.

It is generally conceded that, as a child, you are entitled to sufficient and healthful food, a decent place to live, suitable clothing, adequate medical care, including vaccination against serious diseases, at least eight to twelve years of schooling, the care of parents or parental substitutes, your parents' property if they die without leaving a will, and the protection of the government against exploitation, harm, and discrimination.

In December 1978, a California appellate court gave many children of that state a Christmas present by ruling that any landlord who sought to evict tenants from an "adults only" complex because they had a baby was violating the civil rights of the child.

For the most part, however, the rights of children are goals rather than accomplishments. Most governments have a long way to go before they can even claim to have protected their children from harm, let alone assured them the opportunity to grow up happy, fulfilled, and independent.

YOUR RIGHT TO PROTECTION FROM HARM

One Sunday morning in 1963, some two hundred black worshipers gathered at the Sixteenth Street Baptist Church in Birmingham, Alabama. In the room adjacent to the altar, four young girls were donning their choir robes. Suddenly a deafening explosion blew up the church. Triggered by fifteen sticks of dynamite, it hospitalized twenty people and killed the four choir girls.

They were victims of the race hatred of a Ku Klux Klansman. Another Klansman was asked to comment on the atrocity.

"It wasn't no shame they was killed," he said, adding, "when I go out to kill rattlesnakes, I don't make no difference between little rattlesnakes and big rattlesnakes. . . . I say good for whoever planted the bomb."

Innocent children have frequently been killed and maimed in the bloody feuding between adults. In the constant fighting between PLO terrorists and Israeli forces, both Jewish and Arab children have died. In 1978, during the continuing civil war between North Irish Protestants and Catholics, seven-year-old Jacqueline Hale was shot twice in the back when caught in a crossfire between IRA gunmen and Belfast police. White and black children have died in racial conflicts in Africa.

Embattled adults, in the fire of their passions, are often too intent upon destroying each other to notice or care that children are in the line of fire or at a bombing target.

Ironically, far more children are in even greater danger from adults in their own homes.

Historically, the physical punishment of children has been accepted in many cultures from earliest times. The Bible is often quoted in justification.

"Withhold not chastisement from a boy," Proverbs instructs; "if you beat him with a rod, he will not die. Beat him with a rod, and you will save him from the nether world." Thus the proverb, "Spare the rod and spoil the child."

In olden times, each family constituted a tyranny headed by the father, sometimes benevolently, sometimes not. His word was law. He had the right to punish or abuse any member of his family with impunity.

Archeologists have found the remains of a seven-year-old child of Roman times whose feet were crushed, shoulders bent out of shape, and neck dislocated. In the judgment of scholars, he died of battering, probably by a parent.

Puritan families who emigrated to America considered it a sin for children to complain about their parents. Corporal punishment was widespread, employing birch rods, canes, and leather straps. Not until 1827 did a state—Ohio—get around to passing a law that subjected a father who struck his child to a ten-dollar fine for each occasion.

In 1838, one court proclaimed the state's right to protect children from "neglect or corruption." But states rarely intervened in child rearing. During the nineteenth century, children were regarded as the property of their parents. Foundlings were bought and sold. Child labor was commonplace. Orphans and mentally defective children were experimented upon freely in institutions.

Society was so largely indifferent to the need of children for protection that in 1864, when public indignation was aroused over cruelty toward helpless creatures, it led to the Society for the Prevention of Cruelty to Animals. Not for another ten years did New Yorkers get around to organizing the Society for the Prevention of Cruelty to Children.

With depressing regularity, parents continue to beat, neglect, or sexually abuse their own children. Take the case of the divorced young mother who wanted to go off with a date for the weekend. She freed herself by chaining her little boy to his bed and leaving him a tray of stale sandwiches for his meals.

"Child abuse occurs in all walks of life," declared Dr. Roy Horowitz, who made a study of the problem for the Nassau (New York) County Pediatrics Society. "Doctors and lawyers, too, batter their kids. Ten percent of children under five years of age who come in with trauma are cases of child abuse.... The parent may say that a child slipped when it was really thrown down the stairs. Physicians and nurses tend to buy the story, either because they don't want to believe the parents did it or they don't want to think about it."

Parental use of serious physical violence against children is not at all uncommon. One in five parents, according to a recent study headed by sociologist Richard J. Gelles of the University of New Hampshire, admits having hit children with objects. Over 1,500,000 youngsters between the ages of three and seventeen, Gelles estimates, are physically attacked each year by parents in ways that could cause bodily harm or death.

Psychiatrist David Bakan wrote in the *Journal of Clinical Child Psychology*: "Children have been whipped, beaten, starved, drowned, smashed against walls and floors, held in ice water baths... burned with hot irons and steam pipes... tied and kept in upright positions for long periods... exposed to electric shock . . . buried alive . . . had their limbs held in open fire . . . placed on roofs and fire escapes in such a manner as to fall off; bitten, knifed, and shot."

In 1976, the National Center for Child Abuse and Neglect recorded 2,000 child deaths for which parents were responsible, making this the leading cause of infant mortality.

Yet in only thirteen states can lawsuits be brought against parents on behalf of abused children. Most legislators fear that such suits would destroy family unity or might encourage fraudulent damage suits to collect awards from insurance companies insuring the parents.

Many parents seem incapable of understanding where discipline leaves off and brutality begins. One middle-class father in Washington, D.C., said, "I don't believe in injuring a child or doing him permanent harm, but I know that when I beat the hell out of my kid, it sure clears the air."

A great number of child abuse cases involve children from one to three. Inexperienced young parents often expect too much too soon from infants, treating them as though they were older. Inability to cope with fretful crying wears on the nerves of such parents, who feel guilty and inadequate.

Sometimes it is difficult to draw the line between what constitutes discipline and cruelty. A hard wallop on the backside may be considered abuse of an infant but not necessarily of a teenager. In borderline cases, it may be necessary to assess the whole family situation. How prone is the parent to violence? How often is the child hit, and in what manner? How tense has this made the child?

Child abuse may involve not only beating, burning, whipping, or breaking bones, but also mental violence: persistently frightening or terrifying children, intimidating them, or making them scapegoats for adult problems.

Sometimes the abuse of older children results from a generation gap—the cultural gulf between the generations. A California high school teacher was shocked one morning at the appearance of a pretty fourteen-year-old Vietnamese student who showed up with two black eyes and with her whole face badly swollen. Questioned, she said that her father had beaten her for refusing to get up for family Buddhist prayers at 2:00 A.M., when he returned home from night work.

She had pleaded that she needed her sleep in order to get up early for school. Her father, outraged at his "impudent" daughter's refusal to obey, had "disciplined" her.

The case was referred to Wendy Brown, director of Parents Allied, in Santa Cruz. She explained to the father that in this country a father's wish is not absolute law and that he had no right to beat his children. The girl offered to join the family in daytime prayers if she were excused from the service after midnight. Her father, fearful of deportation, quickly agreed.

Not all cases of abused teen-agers can be so easily resolved. Another fourteen-year-old did not get along with either of her parents. She lived with her father and two brothers after her mother had left home because of the father's brutality. She quarreled with her father constantly about her right to date. Often he exploded and punched her.

The more he abused her, the more she defied him. The more she defied him, the more he abused her. After one savage beating that left her with a black eye and bruises on her cheeks and body, she appealed for help to the Children's Protective Services in Santa Cruz. Director Janet Reed summoned her father and sought to create a better understanding between them so that the girl could return home safe from any more physical abuse.

"No way!" she cried. "I hate him. He'll *never* let me live my own life, and he'll keep on beating me!"

"As long as she lives under my roof," her father snapped, "she'll live by my rules or I'll beat hell out of her!"

Counselor Reed decided that separating the girl from her father was essential. Her mother reluctantly agreed to shelter her for four years, until she was eighteen, and her father was compelled to pay the cost of her support. The solution was not perfect, but at least it ended the warfare between the girl and her father, which could have ended with her in a hospital and her father in jail.

Some fathers have such little control over their emotions

that they may even abuse a daughter sexually. Mothers who are aware that this is happening may prefer to "see no evil" for fear of risking the loss of the family breadwinner by revealing knowledge of his crime. Often the daughter is frightened into submission and silence by a father's violence or his threats.

Most social agencies prefer to resolve nonsexual types of child abuse by voluntary work with the parents, if possible, rather than taking an abusive parent to court. Counselors try to help troubled families find more satisfactory ways of dealing with the problems that cause child abuse or neglect.

Parental neglect, which many people think ranks with child abuse as a serious crime, takes many forms. It may be depriving a child of adequate food, clothing, shelter, or medical attention. It may be leaving small children alone in the house or letting an infant scream or cry without attending to its needs.

Or it may be emotional neglect: failing to touch, care for, play with, love, or provide education for a child. It may be neglecting a child's need of a secure background by raising it in a sordid environment.

Persistent abuse tends to cause a child to lock up feelings of love and trust, the expression of which is needed to form warm human relationships. Such children often remain socially isolated as they grow up.

Some parents commit retarded children to mental institutions without a hearing to judge whether such commitment is advisable. In 1975, a federal district court in Pennsylvania expressed concern over the growing number of such children, committed "so that the other members of his family could go on a family vacation," or because the child "interfered with the routine of the household and disturbed family members."

Some retarded children have been volunteered by their parents for dangerous medical experiments that could not benefit them but that might benefit other children. Theologian Paul Ramsey has criticized such practices as barbarously cruel to handicapped children because they were a "captive population," helpless to prevent this violation of their human rights.

Malnutrition is another serious form of child neglect. According to the UN, half the children in the underdeveloped nations do not get enough food to stay healthy. They suffer from stunted growth, susceptibility to disease, listlessness, and inability to function properly. To a disturbing degree, American children are also affected.

"More than two million pregnant women, infants, and children under four years of age in the United States as of 1970 were undernourished," University of California medical researcher Robert B. Livingston told the Society for Neuroscience, "to such a degree that the brain development of the unborn and young child was in serious jeopardy."

Poverty is a contributing factor but not the sole one. Heavy advertising of "junk" food, which contains little or no nutritional value, has misled some American families into becoming overfed *and* undernourished. In many homes, children's meals and other needs are neglected because their parents are "strung out" on alcohol, pills, or heroin. One young mother became a dealer to pay for her heroin habit. When she sold diluted heroin, a furious customer assaulted her savagely in front of her little daughter. The mother had to be hospitalized for a week. The frightened child, found anemic from malnourishment, was placed in foster care.

In addition to poverty, misleading advertising, and drug addiction, other problems that lead distraught parents to abuse or neglect children are physical exhaustion, unemployment, debt, miserable living conditions, mental illness, and broken marriages.

Neglected and abused children often get into trouble. The tragic story of four-year-old Andre was revealed at a New York University conference on child violence by professor of law Henry J. Foster. Andre was found wandering on the streets of New York and was turned over to the police. When they phoned his mother, she told them, "You keep him. I don't want him."

Found to have chicken pox, Andre was taken to the children's ward of Bellevue Hospital. That night, a baby in the crib next to him began crying while the nurse was out of the ward. Andre took the baby out of the crib. Slamming it against the wall, he dashed it to the floor, killing it.

A psychiatrist found that in Andre's home, whenever he had

cried, he had been told that he was bad. His mother or one of her boy friends had beaten him severely for it. Andre had simply practiced what he had been taught.

Tragically, abused children often grow up believing that violence is the proper way to discipline children or express anger. Having learned by being struck that arguments can be won by the strong using physical force against the weak, they apply this teaching when they, in turn, become parents. Thus child abuse becomes a vicious circle down through the generations.

Yet beating children never really disciplines them. A study of Denver youngsters held as juvenile offenders, conducted by psychiatrist Brandt F. Steele for the National Center for the Prevention and Treatment of Child Abuse and Neglect, found that four out of five had been abused or neglected as small children. Similar studies in New York and California found the proportion to be two out of three. Beatings had taught them only a hatred and defiance of authority.

A recent study in Scandinavia also found that parents who use physical punishment as a major disciplinary tactic have children who are significantly more hostile and aggressive than the children of parents who do not.

Whether a child is screamed at or abused, psychological damage is inevitable. Such children are likely to grow up nervous, fearful, shy, withdrawn, and distrustful, with crippling feelings of guilt and inadequacy.

Some, however, are able to overcome their early handicaps, like noted country singer Hank Snow. But even at sixty-four, according to an Associated Press story, he still winced when he recalled the brutal cruelty of the stepfather who had entered his life when he was eight years old. "I never had a child's life," Hank Snow said.

His painful memories were reactivated in 1976 when he read of the beating to death of a four-year-old girl in Cleveland, Tennessee, by her stepfather. Anguished by the event, he founded the Hank Snow International Foundation for Prevention of Child Abuse and Neglect of Children. As a child, he hadn't reported his own stepfather's abuse of him for fear that his home, unsatisfactory as it was, would be broken up and that he would be taken away from his ill mother and placed in foster care.

If you are an abused child, such a solution may be essential for your safety, at least temporarily. But removing you from your home could inflict a cultural shock that might leave a deep psychic wound. Consequently, child authorities might prefer leaving you in your own home, provided that your parents undergo immediate therapy and that adequate supervision of your home ensures that you will not be abused further.

Sometimes an abusive parent shows every sign of being repentant and assures the counselor that the child will never be beaten again. But if such parents have not really learned how to deal constructively with their own problems, those problems may once again overwhelm them to the point where they lose control and batter their children in frustration.

In 1976, approximately 100,000 American children were removed from their homes to protect them from harm. In many cases when neglect is caused by parents' inability to provide adequately for their children, the state might achieve better results at lower cost by providing financial aid to poor families.

For one thing, not all institutions for children are model ones. For a while, Synanon, the well-known drug rehabilitation center, was considered an excellent refuge for young addicts. Then, in 1978, Julie Moncharsh, fifteen, ran away from the center. In a court deposition, she declared that she "was always being hit. If I did an exercise wrong or changed my sheets wrong, I was hit."

One Synanon official explained, "We just believe in spare the rod, spoil the child."

Abusive or neglectful parents often agree to accept treatment at a counseling center as the price of not having their children taken away. One counselor tells them, "We don't consider you the world's worst people. We're not here to judge you. We're only going to try to help you find other ways to resolve your problems, to make sure that both your children and you are protected from your feelings of frustration and rage. We think you'd like to become good parents, and we want to help."

Parents are taught that there are other, more effective ways of disciplining children than hurting them. A balky small child or one who throws a tantrum may be controlled more easily by holding on to the child's hands or wrists firmly, without inflicting pain, while laying down the law resolutely in words.

Psychiatric technician Patrick Graham of the Child and Family Counseling Center of Santa Cruz has had extensive experience in dealing with unruly children twelve and under. "I've found," he says, "that the intensity of my voice, my facial expression, my communication of anger or displeasure, is sufficient. It makes the point without using violence. It's usually very effective and creates far less resentment in a youngster than being struck."

He added, "If I am *very* angry, I will satisfy my need to strike out by hitting the table or desk near me. That says to the child, 'I'm really angry about this and I want you to stop it.' It usually impresses the youngster. Spanking only satisfies the needs of the spanker rather than the spankee."

In addition to using passive restraint on young children out of control, they can be sent to their rooms for five minutes. Both tactics give a child time to recover from a tantrum.

A study by W. C. Becker, reported in *Review of Child Development Research,* found that aggressive behavior by boys in school can usually be traced to physical punishment inflicted at home. When violence is used against a child, it causes more trouble than it cures.

YOUR FAMILY RIGHTS AS A CHILD

"It's not fair!" eleven-year-old Marya wailed. "All my friends are allowed to go out and play after school. Why do I have to be the only one kept in to practice piano for four hours?"

She ran out the front door, slamming it behind her. When she came home to dinner, there was no food on her plate—only her music lesson book.

"Practice and you eat," said her father. "Not before."

That night Marya ran away.

A few days later, a social worker at the shelter for runaways where Marya had taken refuge called on her parents. He asked why they were so strict about piano practice.

"We come from east Europe," her father said. "We never want our daughter to go through the hardships we did. If she learns to play the piano well, she will always be able to earn a living. We had to scrimp and save to afford the piano and lessons. The least she can do is to practice every day!"

The social worker urged them to take the pressure off Marya by allowing her time for childhood pleasures. Reluctantly, her parents finally agreed to leave it up to her to decide when and how long to practice. Marya returned home.

But soon there was fresh conflict. Her mother insisted upon continuing to choose all of Marya's clothes. Marya refused to wear some new things. "I'm almost twelve," she protested. "You want to dress me like a six-year-old!"

"You're not a woman yet," her mother said. "Don't be in such a hurry to grow up. It's not so great."

Marya grew hysterical. "I won't go to school looking like a baby! All my friends will laugh at me!"

There was a bitter fight. Marya lost her head and called her mother names. Her mother slapped her. Marya slapped her back. Bursting into tears, the anguished girl fled to her room and locked herself in. That night she slipped out the window and ran away again.

Declaring her incorrigible, her parents refused to take her back. Marya had to be placed in a foster home.

As a pre-teen, you need to rebel against parental authority to some extent in order to loosen the apron strings and gradually prepare yourself to take charge of your own life. Nothing is more frustrating than being told that you are too young to make certain decisions for yourself. When you're made to feel powerless, lacking any rights of your own, family ties often seem like chains.

In the sixteenth century, the views of John Calvin prevailed in much of Europe. If you had been born then, your parents would have been led to regard you as having been "born in sin," requiring constant repression, strict control, and hard work to save you from the devil. Play was frowned upon as leading to idle habits.

Calvinist ideas were brought to America by the Puritans. In New England, laws would have upheld the authority of your parents, strictly forbidding you to challenge them. If you defied your parents, you could have been sentenced to death by a court.

In Puritan America, you would not have been allowed to be a child. At a very young age, you would have been forced to work hard and assume responsibilities. As a little girl, you would have combed wool, stored food, looked after poultry, and helped sew, weave, and spin. As a little boy, you would have chopped and hauled wood, watered horses, picked berries, gathered vegetables, and fed the livestock.

For the slightest offense, you would have been punished by birch rods, canes, and leather straps.

You would probably have left your family at a young age to establish your own family. As a girl, you might have married at fourteen. As a boy, having learned to clear woods, shoot game, catch fish, and build log cabins, you would have been eager to leave the family hearth and seek an independent life. As long as there were enough younger hands left at home to do the necessary work, your parents would usually have consented to your early departure.

Opposition to the joyless Calvinist method of raising children came in the eighteenth century from French writer Jean Jacques Rousseau. In an influential work, *Émile*, he advised parents not to insist upon obedience or control of children. They were to stand back and let youngsters develop naturally, learning and maturing by experience.

The movement away from Puritanism led Americans to liberalize child-rearing practices early in the nineteenth century. Foreign visitors were shocked to observe children being given the run of their homes, "tumbling and dragging about books and cushions and chairs and climbing up and down just as they pleased," as one shocked European noted. English visitors were horrified by children who dared quarrel with their parents, insist on foods of their own liking, and shake hands with visitors instead of bowing or curtseying.

One Polish visitor described the five-year-old daughter of his New Jersey host as "a spoiled child, as are most American children.... The least inconvenience that she encounters makes unhappiness for the whole household." A British visitor noted in 1818, "The children are rarely forbidden or punished for wrong doing ... only kindly solicited to do right."

In certain American regions, however, American children were anything but spoiled. The eldest daughter of a Utah Mormon, Hyrum Stratton, recalled, "Discipline was terrible and cruel. Father was unjust and unreasonable in his punishment of the children.... I am sure he never loved his children. He just regarded them as obligations.... And the children were terrified of him.... The change when he came into the house was very noticeable. Usually the younger children all sat on the floor around the room afraid to move when he was there; they were silent until he told them to move. The children were never permitted to eat with their father."

As America's agricultural economy gave way to factories and businesses, fathers went to work for wages. Their absence from home contributed to the erosion of strict paternal control.

During the 1930s, millions of middle-class parents who wanted their children to be achievers raised them according to the ideas of American psychologist John B. Watson. In his book *Psychological Care of Infant and Child* (1928), Watson advised that children, to become successful, had to be raised in an atmosphere that made them independent as soon as possible.

Toward that end, parents were instructed not to respond to children's cries for food or attention, not to coddle, kiss, or fondle them. They were to be held to strict feeding and toilet training schedules. They were also to be given constant tasks to accomplish, as exercises in problem solving.

Watson's "behaviorism" was a modern form of Puritanism. Believers pressured their children to pursue goals they themselves had failed to achieve. High school drop-out fathers insisted that their children go to college.

Music lessons were decreed by parents who dreamed of child prodigies like Mozart, whose parents had pushed him into giving public concerts at the age of five. In the twentieth century, the success of child violinist Yehudi Menuhin made life miserable for many Jewish children, who were forced into daily violin practice.

Rigid control of children was government policy in the communist and fascist nations of the 1930s. "We begin with the child of three," said Robert Ley, chief of the Nazi German Labor Front. "As soon as he begins to think, we press a little flag into his hand. Then comes school, Hitler Youth, the Storm Troops, military service. We do not leave him alone for one minute. When all that is over, the Labor Front comes and takes possession of him again, and does not let him go until death."

Nazi courts took children away from parents who taught them pacifist ideas or who sought to educate them in Catholic convent schools. "The law entrusts German parents with the bringing up of their children," said one court, "only on the condition that they bring them up in the manner that the nation and state expect."

Hitler made no bones about how he wanted them raised. "We take children away from parents," he said. "We bring them up to be new German human beings, and we bring them up thoroughly.... A violent, masterful, dauntless, cruel, younger generation—that is my aim. There must be nothing weak and tender about it."

Hitler Youth were ordered to report to government authorities any anti-Nazi remarks made at home by their parents. Many young zealots did so, leading to their parents' arrest. Parents soon feared to speak freely in front of their own children. The Nazi system sought to turn German boys into fanatical Nazi soldiers, German girls into breeding machines to produce more babies as cannon fodder for Hitler.

In Italy, as well, education was made an important tool of government when Mussolini came to power. Both fascist and communist dictators saw elementary schools as instruments for rearing a new generation of fanatical supporters. Lenin told New York *Times* correspondent Walter Duranty, "Give me four years to teach the children, and the seed I have sown will never be uprooted."

WHO'S RUNNING YOUR LIFE?

In America, in 1945, there was a new voice, that of Dr. Benjamin Spock. In his book *Baby and Child Care*, he advised against an overly strict upbringing. Children thrived far better, he said, in a permissive home where they were given warm affection and where parents followed natural instincts in responding to their needs. Children needed the opportunity to play and do things on their own, Dr. Spock maintained, not follow the rigid direction of parents.

Caribbean families believe in both warm affection and ultrastrict discipline. "West Indians of all classes," David Lowenthal noted in his book *West Indian Society*, "regard children as blessings. Proud to give birth, happy to cherish babies, ready to make sacrifices for a child's future, parents look forward to support and companionship in old age. . . . Upbringing is felt to require physical chastisement; parents regularly resort to the rod."

The situation for children in the American family today is considerably different than in times past. For one thing, most families in our fragmented society realize that parents can no longer count on being taken care of in their old age by children. In addition, the cost of modestly rearing one child from infancy through high school was estimated in 1978, thanks to inflation, to be at least $50,000. Thus, far from being an economic asset to parents, children today represent a heavy expense.

When children arrive without being planned for, some families resent them as both a financial and an emotional burden. When they are welcomed, it is not for any financial benefits they may bring, but for the emotional enrichment they are expected to add to the lives of their parents.

There have also been changes in what is expected of parents. They are no longer required to be everything to their children: nursemaids, teachers, vocational trainers, doctors, and recreational coaches. Society today has eased the burden on parents by providing institutions and trained specialists to share in the care and training of children.

In America today, most state courts recognize the right of a child to be supported, protected, and maintained by parents until he or she reaches the age of at least eighteen.

During the early formative years, adult affection for children is vital to their mental health. In the *American Journal of Psychiatry*, L. Cytryn and D. H. McKnew, Jr. reported that many depressed children they studied "suffered rejection and depreciation by their parents or loved ones . . . at least over a period of many years. Such rejection may take the form of blunt statements, stressing the child's worthlessness or inadequacy, or it may be expressed more subtly through attitudes and actions that indicate a lack of respect, involvement or caring."

Cytryn and McKnew found another right of children often violated with unhappy results—the right not to be overprotected: "Depreciation of the child can be shown through overprotection as well as through rejection; both attitudes convey the same basic message of the child's inadequacy and worthlessness."

As a pre-teen, you need to feel wanted, to be certain of a secure place in your family, and to be able to count on that place tomorrow and next year. Otherwise you may lack confidence in your ability to function well in society.

You may feel resentful or sometimes imprisoned when you are not allowed to participate in activities that a worried parent may consider too dangerous—climbing a tree, diving into a pool, skateboarding, surfing, biking, skiing, going to camp, or just hanging around with certain friends your parents may regard as bad influences on you. You may react by having a violent argument with your parents or feeling so resentful that you want to run away from home or withdraw from your parents emotionally. Sometimes, however, even when a child puts up a fuss after a parent says no, the child may be secretly relieved to be protected by strong, loving parents who will let no harm come to their child. Children constantly test the boundaries of what is permissible for them, expecting parents to draw the line if it is unsafe for them to cross.

There is no doubt that you need to be able, on occasion, to express your feelings of frustration. "Parents need to learn to accept children's expressions of angry feeling, such as 'I hate you,

Mommie. I wish you were dead!' " psychiatric technician Patrick Graham told me. "If too much of a lid is placed upon a child's expression of these feelings, they may explode in forms of violence."

However, parents cannot be expected to tolerate your hitting them, since this suggests that personal violence is an acceptable way of expressing displeasure or disagreement. If you need to ventilate your feelings physically—and you may occasionally—hit a table or chair, not another person. Freedom to express bad feelings makes you feel better and allows you to clear the air. If, however, you feel a *chronic* need to express feelings of hatred toward your parents, obviously something is wrong, and professional help should be sought.

Sometimes parents who are anxious not to be restrictive become excessively permissive. "The permissive parents in my generation have done their children a disservice in agreeing with everything and removing the controls," says noted psychoanalyst Rollo May. "That gives youth more anxiety, takes away their chance to struggle with the older generation, their chance to assert themselves, to test their strength and establish their freedom in a successful struggle against the parent generation."

You also have the right as a pre-teen to feel accepted and be treated as an individual, not pressured to become what you are not. Often a parent indicates disappointment because a child doesn't read enough or reads too much, doesn't go out for athletics or spends too much time in sports, doesn't show an interest in the opposite sex or wants to date too early.

Perhaps the most agonizing words you can ever hear are: "Why can't you be more like . . . ?" All pre-teens are entitled to be themselves. Some parents compel youngsters to "stay neat" by avoiding activities that get their clothes or faces dirty. Such pre-teens may grow up despising themselves as "sissies," hating cleanliness and thinking dark thoughts about parents who consider it more important than having fun.

Another of your rights is that of privacy. The law protects the right of privacy for adults, but not for pre-teens who are old enough to want or need it. Parents may violate it by opening a letter addressed to you, poking into your belongings, eavesdropping on your phone calls, reading your diary, or insisting that you keep bathroom or bedroom doors open.

It is true that parents can learn more about "what's going on" by eavesdropping on your private communications and thoughts. But if they do, they are likely to lose your trust by such unfair tactics.

Betraying your confidence is also a serious parental mistake. One mother complained about not being close to her daughter, who never confided in her. The daughter wrote to columnist Abigail Van Buren, "How can I confide in her when every time I tell her something she tells everybody in town?"

Another of your rights as a pre-teen is intimate communication with your parents or parent substitutes. You are likely to find a few minutes a day given to expressions of mutual affection worth more than a full day spent with a parent who ignores you or who is busy most of the time doing other things.

That concept is increasingly important in these days of high inflation and frequent divorce, because nearly half of all mothers of children under eighteen work outside the home, and one out of every six children now lives in a single-parent family, usually with the mother. "The problem is not one of working mothers," Mary Zuccaro, community educator for Planned Parenthood in Santa Cruz County, told me. "The amount of time a mother spends with a child is not nearly so important as the *quality* of the time spent. Children need parents to show an interest in who they are as people . . . to show them the same respect they expect their children to show them."

Your emotional well-being requires intimate communication with both parents. A study by Rutgers psychologist Donald R. Peterson found that most overly aggressive children have either absent or timid, ineffectual fathers. Most shy children with feelings of inferiority have domineering, self-centered fathers.

Sons need fathers or father substitutes as models for masculine behavior and as towers of security. But daughters, too, need them to help learn safely how to develop a warm relationship with the opposite sex. The daughter lucky enough to achieve such a relationship with her father has an excellent chance of growing up confident of her abilities as a woman.

In some states, if your parents seek a divorce and you are old enough to form an opinion, you are given the right to have your wishes considered when the judge is deciding which parent should be awarded custody. The judge may still rule against your preference if, in his or her view, it is not in your best interests. But at least you are given some voice in a decision that drastically affects your life.

In case of divorce, the one-parent family may not necessarily be tragic for you. You may actually be better off if, when there were two parents present, they were fighting all the time. Studies show that problem children more frequently come from intact homes troubled by family discord and disharmony than from one-parent homes that are peaceful. Of course, the ideal situation is a happy home with both a father and mother present.

All pre-teens have the right to an instructive type of parental control. You need parents to help you control your aggressive feelings, to teach you how to cooperate with others, and to show you how to win acceptance by society.

You are not, after all, an adult and cannot be expected to have the experience or judgment of adults. One child authority, John Holt, takes this view to extremes in his book *Escape from Childhood:* "Children . . . are animals and sensualists; to them what *feels good is* good. They are self-absorbed and selfish. They have little ability to put themselves in another person's shoes, to imagine how someone else feels. This often makes them inconsiderate and cruel. . . . They are always so on impulse rather than by plan or principle. They are barbarians, primitives."

Infants may be frustrated by parental controls that prevent them from pursuing dangerous or undesirable activities. As a preteen, however, you are likely to accept the need for rules of human behavior. You can see the logic of having police to curb crime and violence for the safety of most people. You can also understand the need for parental rules to keep children from hurting one another or from destroying property.

What is expected of pre-teens may depend upon their social

class, according to a study by sociologist Melvin L. Kohn of the National Institute of Mental Health. The trait most often insisted upon by working-class parents is obedience. Middle-class parents seek primarily to encourage achievement.

Working-class parents also tend to punish infractions of rules promptly. Middle-class parents are more inclined to consider children's reasons for such infractions. Daughters in working-class families are more likely to be punished than sons, usually for fighting, disobedience, or other "unladylike" acts.

Parents primarily concerned with controlling children may fail to give them the self-confidence they need to develop a self-reliant attitude toward school and life.

"Kids have the right to be heard, if not necessarily agreed with," Terry Moriarty of Youth Services told me. "Their ideas deserve to be respected. It would also be nice if children could be inspired by parents with the ideal of their own potential. A parent can do a world of good by telling a child, 'You know, you have a talent for this or that. You could really do something with it.' Or just praise the child's ability, and let him or her figure out what to do with it." He added, "Too many parents only abuse children for things they don't like and never think of praising desirable behavior."

Your parents, too, need and deserve some encouragement. When you express admiration for your parents' abilities, you give them a gift far more precious than you may realize.

Open mutual approval between parents and pre-teens creates a spirit of warm family good-will, making each more willing to consider the requests of the other.

There is no firmer bridge between the generations.

YOUR RIGHTS IN PRIMARY SCHOOL

A Kentucky public school recently hired a dietitian, who planned well-balanced lunches. Students were then forbidden to eat lunch anywhere else. When Johnny and his sister Elaine were found eating at a hot dog stand across the way from the school, the principal expelled them.

Their father sued to have the school rule declared in violation of the children's right to eat where and how they pleased. The court ruled in favor of the school.

"Children, if allowed to depend upon their own selection, often indulge themselves in unbalanced diets," the judge said. "Furthermore, if uncontrolled at table, young children are apt to engage in rough or uncouth practices and conduct."

A struggle between you, as a pre-teen, and school authorities ensues in many ways from the time you enter kindergarten. Your desire to follow your own bent is often at odds with the school's insistence that you obey its rules.

Traditionally, teachers have been given almost as much power over children as parents. If you had been a pre-teen in ancient Rome, you would have attended a private school taught by an educated slave. Harsh disciplinarians, these teachers were greatly feared because they had the right to whip students with a rod and did so freely.

If you were a pre-teen in pilgrim America, you would have been expected to learn to read and write at home, taught by parents or by a master to whom you were apprenticed. Because so few pilgrim children learned to read the Bible, however, the Puritans soon set up schools.

Textbooks were carefully selected to emphasize church teachings. Ministers had control of teacher appointments. A 1642 Massachusetts law compelled all children to be taught to "read and understand the principles of religion & the capitall lawes of the country."

If you attended one of the "dame schools," taught by widows or housewives, you could have learned to read Latin as well as English as young as three. After mastering reading, writing, and the catechism, you would have entered a grammar school to study Latin, spelling, grammar, and math.

By 1649, education was obligatory in every New England colony except Rhode Island. In that state, if you were between seven and twelve, you would probably have worked long hours in a mill six days a week. Later on, one Pawtucket firm, Almy & Brown, would have required you to spend your Sundays in school learning the three R's.

Early in the nineteenth century, there was a great influx of European immigrants, and a new role for American schools was visualized. Opportunities for all children were to be equalized through universal, compulsory, free education. Schooling, argued educator Horace Mann, would overcome your handicaps if you were born into a poor family.

But your schools, according to one account, were "for the most part less comfortable, less sanitary and less decent than even the prisons of the day." Often smaller than railroad boxcars, they were poorly heated, drafty, leaking, and dimly lit, with backless benches instead of desks. In western regions, log cabins served as schoolhouses. You would have written with slate pencils on a slate held on your knees.

Most teachers applying for jobs were given favorable consideration if they promised to apply corporal punishment liberally. One school district's qualifications included the ability to "read a chapter in the Testament, teach the Shorter Catechism, and whip the boys."

You would have been disciplined with blows on the palm or other parts of the body with a flat ruler, or your backside or shoulders would have been flogged with a birch rod or hickory switch. Sometimes a knotted rope was used.

One New York State teacher moved about her classroom hitting any children she caught looking up from books they were supposed to be studying. If any children flinched when she looked at them, she generally hit them on the principle that they were feeling guilty about *something* and deserved it.

Emphasis on a schoolteacher's brawn or harshness led to the selection of many who excelled as disciplinarians but were flagrantly inadequate as teachers. A verse scrawled on one Midwestern schoolhouse wall read:

> Lord of love, look down from above,
> And pity the poor scholars.
> They paid a fool to teach this school
> And paid him fifty dollars.

The early courts persistently upheld the right of teachers to use corporal punishment. In 1837, when a North Carolina teacher named Pendergrass whipped one of her pupils with a switch, the child's parents had her arrested for assault. She was convicted but then freed by an appeals court. So long as the student was not maimed, the court ruled, "the master is the judge when correction is required, and of the degree of correction necessary."

Little by little the conviction grew in America that the right of children to an education was not sufficiently guaranteed by simply making schools available. More often than not, when a farming or working-class community had schools, youngsters attended either part time, seasonally, or not at all. If parents needed their children's labor, full-time schooling was considered a luxury that the family could not afford.

So in order to assure the rights of all children to an adequate education, free public schools were widely established and attendance made compulsory. As more and more states passed such laws, resistance grew.

If you were a farm child, your parents would have preferred their own system, whereby they woke you at 4:00 A.M., taught you for two hours, then sent you about your chores.

Some parents complained that public school teachers overworked children by teaching them too much, making them unhappy and more susceptible to disease. In 1859, an article in the *Atlantic* called "The Murder of the Innocents" reported that children were going mad from being required to spend too many hours in class and doing homework. One child was alleged to have perished "insane from sheer overwork and raving of algebra."

Middle-class parents worried that sending their children to public schools would compel them to associate with children of the poor and foreign-born, instead of making friends with their "own kind." They feared that having non-English-speaking students in the schools would lower educational standards. Other parents were concerned that their children would pick up bad manners and immoral thoughts.

In 1859, British philosopher John Stuart Mill also argued against public education as "a mere contrivance for molding people to be exactly like one another: and ... in proportion as it is efficient and successful, it establishes a despotism over the mind."

Throughout the nineteenth century, nevertheless, the free elementary school system spread rapidly in the East. By 1890, Massachusetts required all children six to fourteen to attend school at least twenty weeks a year. Truant officers were sent to homes to investigate the absences of children whose parents kept them out to work in a family shop or store.

Compulsory attendance laws met great resistance from the urban poor in textile centers, where child labor was considered necessary to supplement family income. Many poor families could not afford to buy all their children clothing decent enough to wear to school.

If you were a San Francisco student in the mid-1850s, you would have been sent to a private school or had a tutor. You could have been compelled to spend longer hours in study and fewer in play than public school children elsewhere. Stuffing you with education this way, your parents were led to believe, would teach you to be hard-working and successful in later life.

Rural settlers of the West were by no means convinced that universal education was necessary or desirable. Teachers were few and far between, many little better educated than their pupils. One Montana student wrote in 1863, "Our teacher has just about taught as long as any man can in this town, and consequently is just about played out. The directors hired him at $40 a month. The people got into one of their contrary ways, and kept their children from school."

Opposition to public school education also came from religious groups such as Roman Catholics, German and Scandinavian Lutherans, and Pennsylvania-Dutch Protestant sects, who believed in operating parochial schools of their own.

But the public school system prevailed because most Americans saw it as the most practical, fairest way to provide an education for every child in the country.

The American educational system can boast of fine buildings and apparatus, trained teachers, plentiful books and supplies. Millions of students in primary grades, nevertheless, complain about the way the schools are run.

"Many are saying that the schools are prisons," reports Professor Lawrence H. Fuchs, Brandeis University educational specialist, "where they feel trapped or suffocated.... The schools, by failing to keep pace with the vast changes that have taken place in the total experience of the young, not only fail to relieve the depression of many of them but actually contribute to it."

In Maryland, the Montgomery County Student Alliance declared, "The school system is based upon fear. Students are taught from the outset that they should be afraid of having certain things happen to them—bad grades, punishment from authorities, humiliation, ostracism, 'failure,' antagonizing teachers and administrators—all are things that terrify students as they enter first grade. These fears, which school officials use as a lever from elementary school through high school to establish and maintain order and obedience, have horribly destructive effects."

On the other hand, most parents and teachers believe that strict discipline must be enforced to maintain a quiet, orderly atmosphere in which teachers can impart knowledge. A National Educational Association survey in 1969 found that two out of three elementary school teachers are in favor of "the judicious use of physical punishment in the classroom." Some parents even request that teachers hit their children "whenever they need it."

Other parents strongly object to a teacher's laying a hand on their children. When one parent sued a teacher who did, the Supreme Court dismissed the case. Teachers had a right to inflict corporal punishment for misbehavior, the Court ruled in October 1975, provided that the child was warned beforehand and then punished in the presence of witnesses. Parents who demanded an explanation were entitled to receive it.

As a child in primary school, you may complain because your teachers are too strict and "bossy." Such teachers often feel that it is necessary to be stern in order to control a class and prevent disruptive activities.

The research team of H. H. Anderson, J. E. Brewer, and M. F. Reed studied teachers' classroom personalities. They found that students taught by authoritarian teachers paid less attention and were *more* disruptive and balkier than those taught by democratic teachers. The students who were more mature and socially well-adjusted and showed greater initiative were those whose teachers asked, rather than commanded, them to do things, showed sympathetic interest, and helped them in their tasks.

Yet four out of five public schools permit teachers to punish children physically, often for such misdeeds as "talking out of turn," "not trying hard enough," or "being too aggressive."

Researchers Robert Rosenthal and Lenore Jacobson performed a unique school experiment. Conducting a series of IQ tests among grade school students, they gave teachers the names of those students they said were the brightest 20 percent, as indicated by a computer analysis of the tests. Teachers' attitudes toward those students underwent a distinct change. Almost all of them did far better work than they had ever done before.

The researchers then revealed that those students had not really been rated by the computer. They had simply been chosen *at random* from the whole student body. The teachers, holding higher expectations of them, had communicated a positive attitude toward those students through smiles, eye contact, and nods of approval. As a result, the students, most of whom tested as average and some as below average, forged ahead of their classmates!

Little attention is paid to the personal problems of pre-teens.

"They complain that their teachers are mean," says psychiatric technician Patrick Graham. "When I question them, it usually turns out that their teachers expect them to work harder or longer than they are willing to. Many of these youngsters don't feel capable of coping with schoolwork."

He adds, "Often their problem stems from marital trouble in the home which is disturbing them, or from the pressure of parents' expectations. They can often be helped by a family conference which explores these problems and helps both the parents and children to solve them."

You may have a serious problem in school if you belong to a minority group. Your home background may not have prepared you to meet classroom requirements. For example, many Puerto Rican, Chicano, and foreign-born students who speak little or no English find it impossible to benefit from classes taught in English.

In an attempt to do something about the problem, California ordered any school with at least ten non-English-speaking students or at least fifteen with only a limited command of English in the same grade to offer bilingual instruction.

Similarly, many black youngsters who speak "street" language at home are puzzled by the English used in classrooms. Some urban schools have introduced special classes for them, taught in street language, to make them familiar with "downtown English."

Children's lives can be seriously affected by the labels schools attach to them. Those classified as retarded, disturbed, mentally ill, delinquent, or deprived may be rejected from the regular channels of education and shunted off to special facilities. Made to feel hopeless about themselves, they often give up trying. Expecting to fail, they do.

"By law we are required to establish minimum competency standards for all students," says Joe Blackman, assistant school superintendent for the Santa Cruz (California) School District. "We are not allowed to take individual differences into consideration in reading, writing, and arithmetic."

He adds, "We know that the culturally disadvantaged students won't be able to meet those standards, so the effect of the standards will be discriminatory. A teacher may be sympathetic but still can't exempt minority students from those tests. They will then be labeled inferior or 'deprived' students who need remedial teaching. Many will get discouraged and drop out."

Sociologist Jane Mercer of the University of California led a study of 429 children so classified. It was found that almost half those labeled retarded as a result of school IQ tests were not found to be retarded when studied medically by California's Department of Mental Hygiene.

Many Chicano children had made poor scores simply because they were unfamiliar with the Anglo culture on which the tests were based. Being labeled retarded is not only unfair to such children but also psychologically harmful. They do not do well in school, said a report by the U.S. Commission on Civil Rights, because they attend a school "which either ignores their culture or regards it as an undesirable obstacle to success. Their exclusion very often fosters in Chicano children feelings of inadequacy and inferiority."

University of California educational psychologist Ronald W. Henderson studied children in their homes, working with Mexican-American and Anglo-American first-graders in Arizona. He found that intellectual performance depended on how much the children's parents valued school and learning, particularly the use of language. The best work was done by children whose parents were able to encourage the learning process.

In 1970, a California court ordered schools to test children in their home language and to make efforts to develop tests that youngsters of different cultures could understand.

Schools in Washington, D.C., Kansas City, Los Angeles, and Chicago have adopted a new program called EXCEL, which emphasizes reading, writing, and arithmetic, in addition to discipline—both school-applied and self-applied. Most of the students involved are black. The program is based on the idea of the Reverend Jesse Jackson, who declared that "the choice is theirs: they can put dope in their veins or hope in their brains."

Parents in EXCEL pledge to pick up their children's report cards and make sure they study for two hours a day. Teachers promise to use "all means available" to educate students and instill discipline and respect in them. Students pledge to "push for excellence by striving to learn as much as I possibly can. . . . I will respect the authority of my parents and accept the help of my teachers." The program seems to be working well, according to an official of the Health, Education and Welfare Department.

Recently there has been national anxiety over the fact that many children—not merely those with family problems or belonging to ethnic minorities—go through the school system without learning to read and write adequately. A CBS-TV documentary series in 1978 explored the problem and indicated a number of probable causes.

Children watch too much TV, reducing the time they can spend on books and homework. Often parents are at fault for using TV as a babysitter. Some teachers fail to give regular reading and writing assignments and do not return pupils' papers with mistakes corrected. In many inner-city schools, discipline is poor. Even where principals and teachers have the right to punish students physically, many are reluctant to do so out of fear of being assaulted by a student carrying a concealed weapon or of being sued by angry parents.

Many of the courses of study followed today are also less demanding than they once were, in the view of Joe Blackman, of the Santa Cruz (California) School District. Textbooks are heavily pictorial and use oversimplified language. Film slides and cassettes are frequently substituted for books.

A general decline in scholastic ability has led to pressure from both parents and employers for more rigid demands on students for accomplishment at all levels, especially in the primary grades. They insist that schools must return to concentration on the basics. New and stricter standards of promotion from grade to grade are intended to spotlight earlier children who need special help. Educators must be careful, however, that the return to teaching fundamentals and constant testing do not lead children to feel that the main purpose of study is to get the right answers on multiple-choice tests instead of to understand what they read.

Some parents are dissatisfied with public schools because they feel that their children do not get enough encouraging, individual attention, others because they want their children taught from a religious point of view. A few have attempted to keep their children home and teach them themselves. This invariably brings them into conflict with state educational authorities. That happened to a Mormon living in the state of Washington, when she took one daughter out of the second grade and her other daughter out of the fifth grade to educate them herself.

She held classes for them in the converted garage of their home five hours a day, five days a week, as the law required. But the state brought a lawsuit against her because she did not have a teacher's certification. She argued that she had a right to give her children her own brand of religious instruction. Her children, she pointed out, easily passed the Stanford Achievement Tests given at the end of each school year.

The fifth grader said that she saw her friends after school and did not miss out on social life. Some of her friends envied her freedom from public school. "They think I go to school in pajamas," she said with a laugh. Both girls insisted that they learned far more at home than their friends did at school.

The court nevertheless gave the mother a suspended fine of $100 and ordered her children returned to public school.

We have come a long way from the days when parents were *expected* to teach their own pre-teen children at home. The state today clearly considers that it alone is qualified to set the conditions under which children can be educated.

A group of child coal miners in 1911
(Library of Congress, photo by Lewis Hine)

Children on the canning line in Louisiana in 1911
(Library of Congress, photo by Lewis Hine)

Policemen measuring and weighing boys and girls for working papers in New York City in 1908 (Library of Congress, photo by Lewis Hine)

Small boys of the Hitler Youth gather closely around the lectern as Hitler speaks at the 1934 May Day Rally at Lustgarten. (Photo #306-NT-873-7 in the National Archives)

Students stage a sit-in protest in October 1978 at a Levittown, New York, school to demand an end to the longest teachers' strike in Long Island history. (United Press International)

Protesting the busing of students
in the Boston public schools in 1974
(United Press International)

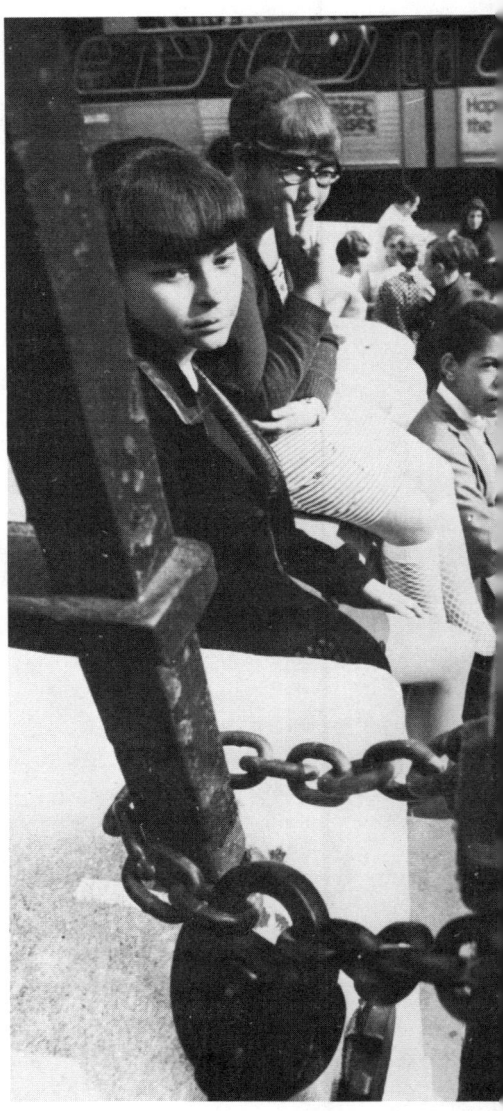

A padlocked gate confronts students during the 1969 city-wide teachers' strike in New York. (United Press International)

Students in Toledo, Ohio, try to rally support for a levy ballot issue to raise funds for their school district. (Wide World)

This poor South Carolina family is being assisted by United States Department of Agriculture food stamps. (USDA photo by Larry Rana)

Children of migrant workers in the New Jersey tomato fields. (USDA photo by Jack Schneider)

Two Pakistani girls do the family laundry at a public water post in Karachi. (UNICEF photo by Mallica Vajrathon)

A young shoeshine boy has to fend for himself on the city streets.
(UNICEF photo by L. Herschtritt)

These are twins at a nutritional rehabilitation center in southern India; the boy (*at right*) was always nursed and fed first, his sister getting what was left over.
(UNICEF photo/Balcomb)

Symbolic of displaced persons all over the world, a young child sits before a barbed wire fence in Algeria. (UNICEF photo by L. Herschtritt)

YOUR FAMILY RIGHTS AS A TEEN-AGER

Janice, sixteen, felt exasperated with her parents. Why didn't they realize they could trust her? If she had wanted to have sexual relations with a boy, she could have done so secretly. She didn't have to go away with her friends for a weekend at the lake just to do that. Why couldn't they understand that all she had in mind was some innocent fun?

"I believe *your* intentions," her mother said. "But at sixteen you just aren't old enough to handle situations like that, Jan. We really wouldn't be good parents to let you take the risk."

"Not old enough, not old enough!" Jan flared. "That's all I ever hear! When *will* I be old enough—when I'm ninety? I'm not a child any more. But that's what you're making me look like to all my friends! 'I can't go—because Mommy and Daddy won't let me!' " Her voice broke. *"Please* . . . you've got to let me go. It's very important to me!"

"No," her father said. "For your own good, Jan."

"Thanks a million!" She stormed off in tears.

On Saturday morning, she slipped out of the house early with a small overnight bag and went off on the weekend with Donald and six other couples. A note she left behind said, "Please try to understand. I *had* to go. Don't worry, I won't do anything you don't want me to."

She had a miserable time. Feeling guilty about disobeying her parents and worrying about it, Jan couldn't relax and enjoy the weekend. It didn't help matters when three couples paired off overnight and Donald pressured her to do likewise. When she refused, he turned sullen and ignored her.

Jan's return home met with angry reproaches that reduced her to tears. For one month she was restricted to the house and "grounded"—forbidden to ride in any teen-ager's car.

Relations between Jan and her parents were strained during most of the punishment period. They remained shocked that she could have disobeyed them so flagrantly. She was mad at them for not having trusted her to go on the trip, mad at herself for having disobeyed and gone, mad at Donald for behaving as immaturely as her parents had predicted.

In early America, adolescents were expected to leave home at a much younger age than they are today—girls through marriage, boys through apprenticeship to a trade. Both were eager to end their childhood and assert their independence. Teens matured earlier because they were expected to. Many considered home not a place to remain, but a nesting place to leave as soon as possible.

If you were a boy, it would not have been unusual for you to go to sea at the age of fourteen, like Nathaniel Hathorne (the father of Nathaniel Hawthorne), who became captain of his own ship at twenty-one. Grover Cleveland, going to work as a store clerk at fifteen, declared that adversity was good for him and that he enjoyed the struggle to get ahead in life on his own.

"If you are talented and work hard," *McGuffy's Readers* told boys of that day, "you are bound to get ahead in America."

If you were a girl, you had fewer job opportunities. You might have worked as a seamstress, dressmaker, or laundress. In 1820, New England mills began hiring young girls to work the looms, and soon many were also employed as shopgirls. For the most part, the only real security offered you would have been in marriage, with the understanding that you had to be subservient to the husband who supported you and devote your life to raising children.

The twentieth century largely reversed the policy of early independence for teen-agers. One reason was the desire of labor unions to delay the entry of young people into the labor market. Fewer workers meant higher wages. So organized labor supported legislation to compel teen-agers to remain in school longer. As a consequence, many felt frustrated at being kept at home under parental thumbs during middle and late adolescence.

Puberty does more than bring about sexual maturation. This change in the body is frequently accompanied by powerful emotional turmoil that may result in conflict with other people, particularly parents. Teens feel misunderstood and rebellious and often agonized by guilt over uncontrollable outbursts of temper.

Parents, too, are likely to be upset when their formerly obedient child suddenly balks, questioning their decisions and challenging their authority. They may also be secretly saddened by this reminder that maturity is setting in and that the day is not far off when they will "lose" their child.

Teens, in turn, feel ambivalent about becoming independent. On one hand, it means the delicious freedom of running their own lives. But, on the other, it means giving up the security they have long enjoyed as children in exchange for adult responsibilities and pressures.

Nevertheless, teens invariably echo common complaints: "My parents treat me like a baby," "I don't get to make my own decisions," "I'm not allowed to do what I want to do when I want to do it," "They expect too much from me," "They don't realize times have changed since they were teen-agers," "They don't understand how out of it you are if you can't do things other kids do," "Parents always nag and order you around," "I'm sick and tired of being ordered to clean my room all the time."

In some respects, it's harder to be a teen-ager in this generation than in those past. Formerly, there was much greater agreement about right and wrong, so a teen's choices of behavior were simpler. For a great many people, young and old, today, moral values seem to be in flux.

Many teen-agers are unwilling to listen to parents who refuse to recognize that times have changed. Many parents, in turn, believe that there are moral principles that have *not* changed and regard some of the actions of teens as reckless and irresponsible.

It is tragic when teens and parents fail to discuss their differences and try to compromise, because such failure leads to alienation. What each group needs is esteem and approval from the other.

Teen-agers frequently resent being treated like children yet expected to act like grownups. One seventeen-year-old Minneapolis youth quarreled with his father, who refused to hear of his desire to join the Peace Corps.

"I used to have do-good ideas like that when I was a kid, too," his father scoffed. "I outgrew 'em, thank God, and so will you. You're not here to waste your life on a bunch of gooks who were born poor and ignorant, and will die that way. Your job is to make something of yourself, like I did!"

The boy asked his school guidance counselor miserably, "How can I respect my father if he shows no more understanding of how I feel than that?"

A fifteen-year-old Dallas girl complained, "All my parents want me to do is to agree with them or shut up!"

In the power struggle between teens and parents, the law has given parents most of the cards. As long as young people are legal minors, they have no right to control their own educational choices, where or when they work, how they use money, their religious choices, their recreation, the clothes they wear, what they eat, where they sleep, and a host of other choices that all adults have.

Conflict is inevitable over these choices as young people

grow up and seek a greater voice in running their own lives. Adolescence involves a series of progressive skirmishes to persuade parents to surrender more and more of their authority. They tend to resist out of fear that their teen-agers are not yet ready to use wisely the greater degree of autonomy they demand.

Betty, sixteen, got a summer job at a drive-in eating spot that required its waitresses to wear tight white sweaters. Her father, asked to drive her to the job on his own way to work, refused. "Dressing like that will give men the wrong idea about you," he said. "I won't have it!"

Betty's tears availed her nothing. The result was that she had only a few babysitting jobs that summer and spent most of her time with a group of teen-agers who popped pills. The boys ran afoul of town police by breaking into a beach house. Betty was among the girls detained with them. When her father was summoned to the police station, Betty listened impassively to his angry reproaches.

"Well," she replied coldly, "at least I'm not working at a drive-in in a form-fitting sweater, right?"

Daughters generally have a more difficult time than sons in exercising control over their dating patterns.

"I know my parents mean it for my best interests," says a fifteen-year-old Hartford, Connecticut, girl, "but lots of times they just don't know what they're talking about. They may get uptight about the looks of a boy who's really a nice person, yet think it's safe for me to date a smoothie who's bad news!"

One seventeen-year-old Denver girl told a researcher, "The worst part about parents is they just don't trust you. They read something about how many kids are sleeping around, so every time you go out on a date they're afraid you're having sex. They won't let you go to a drive-in movie because you might have sex in the car. And they order you home by eleven, as though that would stop it if you really wanted to. Sometimes you feel tempted to do it so they don't waste all that worry for nothing!"

Nothing chafes teens like having to be home from dates at an early hour, but parents often feel that the recreation that occupies the early part of the evening on most dates, such as a movie, sports event, or dance, is nonsexual, whereas later hours free a young couple for sexual activity.

Abel, seventeen, fought with his parents when they insisted that he had to be home from the junior prom half an hour earlier than his date had to. "We're being liberal enough as it is," his father said. "The door will be locked at twelve-thirty. If you're late, don't bother coming home."

Abel angrily took up the challenge. Instead of coming home, he went to sleep at a friend's house. After a few days, and some hints by his friend's parents, he finally had to go home. His father refused to speak to him. Relations between them soured. Abel couldn't wait until his graduation the following year, so that he could take a job and leave home.

Many teen-agers also complain of pressure by parents for achievement—higher grades, winning prizes, earning a place in the band or on a school team, getting scholarships, and the like. Sometimes parents may be selfishly motivated, seeking an ego trip in the personal status that comes with having successful children. More often they simply want their teens to enjoy the pride and opportunities that achievement brings.

Nevertheless, parents often fail to realize that such pressure tends to make teen-agers tense and anxious, as well as feel guilty and inadequate if they disappoint parental expectations. Parents can accomplish more for teens by simply offering the unqualified love and support they need for gaining the self-confidence to undertake achievements on their own. In our highly competitive society, teens already have more than enough outside pressures driving them to excel.

Another form of parental pressure is the kind that requires a teen-ager to assume adult responsibilities too soon. Today, with the majority of mothers working outside the home, teen-age girls are doing a lot of marketing and cooking. Statistics show they spend *one out of three* of the family food dollars every month.

In one four-child home where both parents worked, thirteen-year-old Jenny was expected to serve as a stand-in mother, cooking, doing housework, and looking after smaller brothers and a sister after school. Overwhelmed by trying to keep up with schoolwork, friendships, and the expectations of her parents, Jenny fell into a deep depression.

She ran away from home and found refuge in a teen-age shelter. "I can't be a mother to my brothers and sister," she told the counselor, weeping. "I need a mother myself!"

"Running away," observed the Reverend Larry Beggs of San Francisco's teen refuge Huckleberry House, "is often an attempt to cause parents to face a problem which they continually refuse to acknowledge." So, often, is a teen-age suicide attempt.

Some 5,000 young people between fifteen and twenty-four commit suicide each year, and many thousands more make the attempt unsuccessfully. It is an alarming problem. Adolescents often take setbacks harder than adults and act out their frustrations more dramatically.

Three types of home situations may predispose unhappy teen-agers to run away or in extreme cases to attempt suicide. The first involves parents who, busy pursuing their own lives, may make their teen-agers feel neglected or rejected. Some parents are withdrawn because of mental illness or excessive use of alcohol or drugs. In homes broken by divorce, teens may feel responsible for the break-up or simply lost in a new family situation.

The second home situation involves parents who may seek rigid control of adolescents and make excessive demands upon them. Living only for and through their children, they leave youngsters little opportunity to explore and find their own identities.

The third home situation involves parents in troubled marriages. Their children, exposed to daily marital fighting or bitter recriminations, suffer great nervous strain. Many are made even more miserable if one or both parents take out their frustrations on their children and make them scapegoats.

In such situations, teen-agers who need help can find it by a free phone call to the National Runaway Hotline at 800-621-4000 (in Illinois, 800-972-6004). It operates on a twenty-four-hour free and confidential basis. Some communities also have teen-age resource centers, which provide counseling for troubled youngsters, including those desperate enough to contemplate suicide.

Life can be agonizing for you as a teen-ager if you live in a home where one or both parents are alcoholic.

"The children are brutally buffeted in the mounting turmoil," observes Harry Milt in his *Revised Basic Handbook on Alcoholism*, "and struggle to maintain their sanity, sense of security and identity, but this is impossible. Sooner or later . . . emotional disturbances show up, or else psychosomatic illness. If the children are old enough, they may begin 'acting out' by running away from home, failing in their schoolwork, stealing, becoming sexually promiscuous."

When the alcoholic parent refuses to seek help or be helped, it may not be fair to the children to keep them imprisoned in such an environment.

Life can also be difficult for you as a teen-ager if you live in a home run by a dictatorial father. One father, a military man, declared, "My kids have the right to do as *I* think best. When they're finally out from under my roof, they won't have to take my orders. Until then, they damn well do."

Parents who strike teens inadvertently teach them that this is the way to deal with other people in society who may differ with them. Some teen-agers suffer constant verbal abuse from parents. Either type of humiliation can make them feel worthless, bringing on depression or mental illness.

Most of the youngsters who run away from home, surprisingly, come from middle-class families. Some are teen-age girls whose mothers have married a second time and who feel unwanted or rejected by their stepfathers. They are looking for some acknowledgment of their lovability that they can't get from their mothers alone. They miss the attention of a father, or father figure, to teach them how to relate to men.

The lack of a mother's love can also be devastating to a girl. Take the case of Carolyn, as reported by *Newsweek* in 1978. Carolyn was twelve when her parents were divorced. At thirteen and fourteen, feeling that her remarried mother no longer loved her, she swallowed an overdose of sleeping pills several times. Once she had to be hospitalized for over half a year.

Later she climbed a bridge, threatening to jump off, but was talked down. Next she drank a whole bottle of vodka, then staggered out on a highway in front of cars. When Carolyn was fifteen, her mother could bear no more. Washing her hands of the problem, she threw Carolyn out of the house.

A 1964 study led by A. Robey, reported in the *American Journal of Orthopsychiatry*, found that many girl runaways had mothers who failed to provide them with needed affection.

"Society is not attaching as much importance to the runaway problem as it should," said Officer Warren McGuinness of New York City's runaway squad. "Far too many youngsters are being driven from home, away from responsibility and away from educational development, into the street."

All teen-agers need to feel that there is a safe place where they belong, where they can count on being cherished and cared for by parents or parent substitutes, where they can feel loved despite the mistakes that every one of them makes.

Runaways, in their immaturity, frequently imagine that being on their own will bring them independence. But as minors they can't get food stamps or medical aid or rent an apartment. And jobs aren't easy to come by for teen-agers. In effect, they find themselves just as dependent as ever, but on adults other than their parents.

Many teen-agers who run away don't really want to leave home but simply do so to dramatize their unhappiness. They hope their flight will make their parents feel guilty and repentant, ready to change home conditions they find intolerable.

There would certainly be less unhappiness if more parents gave teens the attention they need and lent a sympathetic ear. Fathers, in particular, need to make time to be fathers, not just breadwinners.

Instead of listening to teens, many parents just scold or nag. Often they are merely trying to keep their children from making the same mistakes they did. But adolescents eventually must be given the right to live their own lives and make their own mistakes. We learn best how to avoid pitfalls when we stumble into a few.

The most successful parents are those who manage to draw the fine line between being overprotective and overpermissive. As children grow up, good parents try to instill in them a code of conduct and a series of values, then trust their children to act in compliance with them. They make an honest effort to see situations through their youngsters' eyes. If a parent knows that something a child wants to do is too risky and a discussion of the reason fails to settle the matter, the parent may then find it necessary to say, "Well, *I* consider it a bad idea, and I'm sorry if you're disappointed, but the answer is still no." If young people know that their parents have treated them fairly all along, allowing them to make some decisions—and mistakes—on their own, they are more likely to accept the checkmate, secretly relieved to have the danger signs posted.

Young people mature more rapidly when they practice "futuristic thinking": taking into consideration any future options they may close off for themselves by choosing immediate gratifications. Their parents can help them clarify these choices.

For example, if you're an eighteen-year-old thinking of marrying right after high school, you would be wise to reflect deeply on a parent's reminder that this will cost you the option of going to college and perhaps foreclose your opportunity to enter the profession of your choice. You might think about your parents' advice that, however hard it is to hold off, it's even harder to raise a child when the rest of your friends are going to college or enjoying themselves on ski weekends.

Some teen-agers might display impatience with such "parent talk" while at the same time feeling grateful for wise advice.

"We're not going to act like we're listening to it, or like we think it's great," one sixteen-year-old Boston girl told a teen-age rap group, "but we still want to hear it. That doesn't mean we won't give them a hard time anyway. We'll listen, argue, then make up our own minds."

As you show increasing signs of maturity, if your parents are wise, they will gradually increase your right to make significant decisions.

"The worst thing a parent can do to you," said a fifteen-year-old Chicago boy, "is tell you to grow up all the time, but keep on treating you like a little kid."

Fran, sixteen, felt smothered by her parents' protection. Refusing to recognize that she was growing up, they lavished on her the same concern and protection that they had when she was a little girl. She was not allowed to go away to camp—"the food is unhealthy." She was not allowed to take trips with friends—"too many crazies attacking girls alone." She was forbidden single dates—"that's how girls get pregnant."

Her mother, who had no interests outside the home, burdened Fran with such avowals as, "I live only for you."

Fran fell into an acute depression, which brought the family into counseling. The therapist found her mother fearful of the day Fran would leave home, ending the parental role outside of which the parents' marriage had no meaning. Fran was found to be ambivalent herself about growing up. She had accepted babying to postpone the day of adult responsibility.

The situation improved when all members of the family understood the problems involved. The father eased his wife's apprehension by working less and spending more time with her, reviving their neglected companionship. The mother, relieved, no longer felt the need to cling to her "baby," and Fran was permitted to go out more. As her life grew more normal, her depression vanished and she welcomed maturity.

Many parents today, afraid or unable to impose arbitrary rules or values, withdraw from the question of discipline. Fathers often leave it up to mothers, who sometimes feel unable to cope, especially with older children. By default, both often let children's peer groups dictate to their offspring what they will wear, how they will behave with the opposite sex, where they will go, and what they will do. Lacking family guidelines, many young people yield to the pressures of their crowd. They are frequently unhappier for it.

Reverend C. Galea asked boys confined in the Guelph Correctional Center to draw up a code for parents that they wished their parents had followed. The code urged in part: "Bug us a little. Be strict and consistent in dishing out discipline. Show us who's boss. It gives us a feeling of security to know we've got some strong supports under us."

It went on, "If you catch us lying, stealing, or being cruel, get tough. Let us know WHY what we did was wrong. Impress on us the importance of not repeating such behavior. When we need punishment, dish it out. But let us know you still love us, even though we have let you down. It'll make us think twice before we take the same move again.... And don't be intimidated by our threats to drop out of school or leave home. Stand firm.... Kids don't want everything they ask for."

For teen-agers, honest self-evaluation is an important first step in trying to establish a good rapport with their parents. This doesn't mean putting yourself down. It involves trying to think about yourself with detachment, recognizing your good points but also ways in which you may improve. Immature traits such as recklessness or unreliability may be making it more difficult for your parents to accommodate your changing needs.

It makes sense to strengthen these weak points, to impress your parents that you are ready for greater freedom. Angry defiance is not the best way to persuade them. Parents are more likely to be sympathetic when you explain quietly and honestly why a decision of theirs is making you miserable.

Boys particularly need to recognize that it's perfectly masculine to be sensitive, to reveal hurt feelings. Communication with parents is difficult when they feel too "proud" to admit how they feel because of the sexist myth that males are always strong, tough, independent, and assertive.

Teens expect parents to listen but often forget to return the compliment. Parents need to be understood, too. They are only human—often indecisive, at times ambivalent, scared, or unsure of themselves. Parenting is a tough job, with lots of hard problems. It's all too easy to make mistakes.

Meanwhile, there are agencies that stand ready to help both teens and parents who have not achieved a good rapport.

You may find a discussion of your problems with your school counselor helpful. He or she can also refer you to agencies in your community that specialize in teen-age conflicts. Such agencies are usually listed in the yellow pages of your phone directory under Social Service and Welfare Organizations, Community Counseling, and Adolescent Crisis Services.

There may also be a hot line, a telephone listening service manned by teen-agers that troubled youngsters can call to get problems off their chests, discuss difficulties, and get advice.

Teens can also discuss their problems with a priest or minister, who may be able to influence their parents.

Parents having problems with children can get the same kind of help by checking yellow-page listings under Social Service and Welfare Organizations, Family Counseling Services, Community Counseling, and Parents' Centers.

Some teens see the use of a family car as their right. Often there is conflict over the times when it may be used, with whom it may be shared, the curfew for returning home, and other rules for its use.

Sitting behind the wheel of a car makes teens feel independent, powerful, and mobile. Their lack of adult experience, ability, and judgment, as indicated by higher accident and insurance rates, often makes parents uneasy about the extent of teen-age driving they permit.

No teen-ager has a "right" to use a family car. It is a privilege that parents grant when they are convinced that you can be safely trusted behind a wheel, after being trained in defensive driving.

One father lost two sons who crashed in a family car while speeding in a drag race at eighty miles an hour. "It was my fault," he said bitterly. "I was so anxious to have my sons think of me as a nice guy that I let them fool around with the car, even after I had reports that they were speeding recklessly."

Teens have the right to expect parents to protect them from dangerous situations. "Kids who get in trouble," family counselor

Mary Zuccaro told me, "often wish parents had given them more discipline, shown enough concern to want to know where they were and when they were coming home."

With justification, you have a right to expect a fair and sympathetic hearing for all your family requests, but you also have an equal responsibility to understand some of the concerns of your parents.

If, as a minor, you accidentally hurt someone or damage property, your parents are legally responsible for damages. If you get into trouble with the law, your parents will be called to account. If you make a serious mistake of any kind, society expects your parents to come to your rescue. You are not legally responsible for your actions until the age of adulthood, which most states now set at eighteen.

Moral responsibility comes earlier. Parents expect to see signs of it when they grant special privileges, such as use of the family car. If you're responsible, you'll replace the gas you use, check the oil, radiator, and tires, and won't beg off to go swimming or play ball when the car needs washing.

Because today a large number of Americans no longer accept the rigid moral principles of the past, many parents have been faced with new questions about your rights as a teen-ager. Do homosexual teens, for example, have the right to parental understanding and support? Or must they submit to parental demands that they undergo counseling or therapy to change their sexual orientation?

Adolescent homosexual experiences may simply be a phase of sexual development some teens pass through, but on the other hand, adolescent experience in this area may well be the thing that triggers a whole lifetime of homosexual orientation. If a teen-ager is uncomfortable or troubled about it, or if it triggers constant family conflict, counseling should then be sought, as for any other problem causing great difficulty.

Do you have the right to be allowed to smoke, to drink, use pot, PCP (angel dust), or other drugs?

A parent who gives you permission to smoke marijuana or

use drugs or to drink if you are under the age set by law is telling you that it is all right to break the law. Whether you agree with these laws or not, and no matter how many teens and adults ignore them, if you decide to violate them, you must be prepared to accept the prescribed punishment if caught.

A recent study by the National Institute on Drug Abuse found that one in eleven high school seniors smokes pot daily. One medical study in 1978 disclosed that after three months of smoking one joint a day, your lung tissues can be damaged and some brain processes permanently impaired. Other studies have found pot relatively harmless; the subject is still controversial. Injecting a hard drug like cocaine, however, can cause convulsions, insomnia, nausea, and severe headaches. An overdose can kill you.

Between 1970 and 1976, about 2.5 million arrests involved marijuana. In Jefferson City, Missouri, one young girl went to jail for five years for purchasing an ounce of pot and selling half to her date, who proved to be a narcotics agent.

From 1977 to 1978, the use of the narcotic drug PCP doubled among youngsters aged twelve to seventeen, according to the National Institute on Drug Abuse. The drug, marketed legally as an animal tranquilizer, is a powerful neurotoxin that can cause psychotic behavior, convulsions, and death.

One California twelve-year-old on PCP became irrational and aggressive. Throwing emotional fits, he punched and injured his mother. In juvenile court, he threw an uncontrollable tantrum before the judge and was institutionalized.

Some young teens seek the thrill of getting high by sniffing glue or paint fumes without realizing the danger. "They won't," Assistant District Attorney Robert M. Patterson told me, "until some future time when, if they keep it up, part of their brain is burned away."

As for smoking at any age, and drinking when old enough to meet state requirements, one father told his teen-age son and daughter, "You have a legal right to do both, knowing that smoking can cause cancer, emphysema, and heart trouble, and that drinking can cause cirrhosis of the liver and alcoholism. The choice is yours. It depends upon how much you value your health."

You have the right to as much freedom of choice as you can safely handle. The question is: how much is safe?

Family arguments over how much to relax controls over teens are natural and healthy. But actions speak louder than words. You can prove to your parents that you are responsible enough to be trusted more by taking care of your household chores without having to be reminded, by returning home when you say you will or phoning if late, by doing homework conscientiously, and by being helpful to younger brothers and sisters.

Parents who fail to acknowledge such signs of maturity and act more like police than parents are likely to be asking for trouble rather than preventing it.

Parent-teen relations in America have not kept pace with all the changes in life style that have taken place in the last decade. Perhaps the next generation will see less order giving by adults, less shouting by teens, and more reflective discussion of their differences and compromise by both.

YOUR RIGHTS IN JUNIOR HIGH AND HIGH SCHOOL

Two teen-age boys were proud of the comic decorations for the senior dance they'd spent a great deal of time and effort creating. But the faculty adviser for the dance commented nervously, "I don't know, fellas. They're a bit risqué."

The boys produced two girl classmates who agreed that the decorations were funny and inoffensive and would be a great hit. But the assistant principal took one look and said, "Nothing doing. Those decorations are out." Dismayed, the two seniors tried to argue. The assistant principal snapped, "You heard me! I said they're out, and that's that!"

As he turned to leave, the two youths, frustrated, made derisive gestures toward him. He saw them.

"All right, you wise guys," he flared. "You're suspended for five days. And I want to see your parents!"

Upset, the boys asked their faculty adviser to intercede for them. He went to the principal, who agreed that if the boys wrote a letter of apology to the assistant principal, the school would not notify their parents or note the suspension in their school records. They wrote the letter.

The assistant principal refused to be appeased. Making copies of their letter, he placed one in each boy's file record, sent a copy each to their parents, and distributed others to their teachers and other school personnel.

One of the boys told his parents, "I know you're upset because we insulted the assistant principal. But we were promised that if we apologized, the school wouldn't involve you or punish us any further. They broke their agreement!"

His parents went over the principal's head to the county assistant superintendent in charge of high schools. That official agreed the school had been wrong. He rescinded the two days of the boys' suspension that still remained and ordered all references to the incident stricken from their records.

The principal protested. "How can we maintain discipline if the authority of the school isn't upheld?"

"It shouldn't be upheld when the school is wrong," the assistant superintendent replied. "In this case the school violated its agreement with the two students. To uphold that violation would be to teach students not to trust the word of authorities."

More and more students and parents today are becoming aware of student rights that schools may not ignore. They are also beginning to question the way schools are taught and run.

The first American high school appeared in Boston in 1821. It was patterned after the European *Hochschule*, which was organized to make trade and occupational skills available outside the apprenticeship system. But even by 1870, there were only enough high schools in the nation to enroll 80,000 students. Almost all of them were boys.

Between 1820 and the Civil War some two hundred "finishing schools" were established to prepare girls to win husbands, run homes, and rear families. Refined manners, hemstitching, and needlework were the principal studies. When Susan B. Anthony insisted upon learning long division, none of her instructors would teach it to her. One New York school that taught girls geography provoked shocked protests that such "unfeminine" pursuits would end up destroying the fabric of family life.

Public high schools developed slowly in the United States during most of the nineteenth century. They were regarded much as we regard colleges today: as seats of higher education not essential for the average young American entering the working world. In 1870, with one out of five Americans unable to read or write, the emphasis was still on literacy.

Of the relatively small number of teen-agers who graduated from high school, as few as one in ten went on to college. The universities were filled mostly by young people from wealthy families who were prepared by private secondary schools. Nevertheless, the curriculum of public high schools was in large measure set by college entrance requirements instead of being geared to the needs of most students.

Immigration brought a tremendous increase in demand for public high schools. In the period from 1890 to 1896, public high school enrollment almost doubled. Few teachers, however, were college graduates. College graduates could command much higher salaries in the business world. For much of the twentieth century, the quality of public high school education, therefore, did not measure up to that of wealthy private secondary schools that could afford higher teacher salaries.

Our public high schools today still have many problems, as indicated by the high drop-out rate, estimated at approaching 10 percent a year. The reason most often given for dropping out is boredom with the curriculum.

Many students today find the subjects they are forced to study irrelevant to their lives. One fifteen-year-old Arizona girl who planned to be a hairdresser objected to studying geometry and dissecting frogs in biology as a waste of her time.

"I'm not interested in those subjects," she complained. "I'll never use them in my life. So why do I have to be made miserable in school by spending so many hours, and sweating out exams and finals, on stuff I don't care anything about? I've got enough pressures in my life without that!"

"The public school as an institution for educating children is rapidly becoming obsolete," thinks Dr. James C. Craig, assistant superintendent for instructional and pupil services for Montgomery County, Maryland. "For the most part its programs are dull and boring, intellectually sterile, and almost totally unrelated to the real concerns of youth, or to the concerns of society outside of school."

Poor teaching methods and large classes are part of the problem. Many teachers see not a roomful of individuals sitting before them, but only a blur of young faces. The result is often assembly-line education instead of individualized pupil-teacher relationships that can strike sparks within students and inspire them with new ideas and horizons.

The lack of such a relationship can also work hardships on students with time problems. Many need to work after school or have night jobs. When they can't do all the outside schoolwork demanded of them and ask for understanding or extra time, they are often told, "Sorry, I can't make exceptions."

"You just stick your head in a buzz-saw if you try to buck the system," a senior in a Dallas school said resentfully. "All they want you to do is what you're told and not make waves. Eat when you're told, go to the john when they let you, show up in class between bells, and go home when the last bell rings."

Some teachers seem to exercise power unfairly by giving a lot of daily homework, as though students had no other assignments to do. "My English teacher lays two hours' homework a day on us," complained a seventeen-year-old California girl. "I've got to shop and do housework for an invalid lady three afternoons a week. The result is I often don't get to bed before midnight. It's all I can do to stay awake in classes!"

Many teen-agers protest the pressure they're put under by the grade system. "I'm less interested in learning anything than in memorizing the right stuff to get good marks on tests," said a sixteen-year-old Nebraska boy. "When I freak out and get lousy grades or flunk, my parents ground me."

Instead of inspiring the desire to learn, school systems often turn out students who are apprehensive, nervous, and concerned with marks and passing tests instead of gaining knowledge.

Minority students were supposed to get an upgraded brand of education when the courts ordered busing to integrate formerly all-white schools. But in many communities integration took place on a token basis, leaving schools still largely black, like those in Washington, D.C. A Rand Corporation study in 1978 revealed that the chief result of court-ordered desegregation was widespread "white flight" to the suburbs.

When one student graduated from mostly black Roosevelt High in the top 20 percent of her class, she still had to be admitted to Georgetown University as a "special student on a noncompetitive basis" because her combined college entrance exam scores were below the acceptance level of 610. And the highest score she was able to obtain while attending college was a failing 380 in English. Within five months she had to drop out, saying that she felt "cheated, hurt, and surprised" to find that her high school education had left her so wretchedly unprepared for college.

This problem doesn't affect minority students only. Many teen-agers in high school read at a sixth grade level, and three out of five students have some kind of reading problem. Some of these students drop out in discouragement and then return to school only to drop out again. Attempts to compel bored, failing students to remain in school sometimes result in violent disruption of classes.

School authorities sometimes agree with students who complain that their high schools provide unsatisfactory curriculums.

When Ed, fifteen, was questioned by a truant officer as to his reasons for being constantly absent from classes, he replied, "It's all a lot of garbage. I'm not interested in any of it. Why do I have to sit there and be bored six hours a day?"

Pressed, he agreed reluctantly to attend continuation school. But after less than a week he dropped out. Then, one day soon after he had turned eighteen, Ed visited the computer center of a local community college, which permitted the public to use its computers. Fascinated by them, he became eager to study electronics, to the delight of his parents.

The college agreed to accept him as a student, provided his high school would consent. The school refused. Ed, the principal insisted, would have to return, complete his courses, and graduate first. Ed and his parents appealed to the assistant superintendent of schools, who sent a letter to the college giving Ed permission to matriculate, even though the high school principal was outraged and felt that school authority had been undermined.

Perhaps the moral is, if high school bores you, try college! Many students do, in fact, find college far more enjoyable.

If you're a typical high school student, you would probably prefer a less structured curriculum—one that would give you a freer choice of subjects and include many subjects now not taught. One Albany, New York, senior asked in an essay, "What makes one generation think that the same subjects it studied twenty years ago are appropriate for the new generation, when the world keeps changing?"

Scientific knowledge, especially, is developing so fast that today's technical knowledge may be obsolete in just a few years. Students need to be taught theory and fundamentals that can help them absorb new developments and apply them to changing conditions.

"What seems to me a much more serious problem," observes sociologist Gordon Rattray Taylor, "is our present failure to teach young people how to cope with life. We teach them nothing about themselves or their identities—and little enough about how to maintain their bodies in a healthy state, let alone their psyches. They learn nothing about the psychological differences between individuals, and between the sexes. . . . But above all we should teach people how to try to be happy."

Many school authorities, teachers, and parents are reluctant to give students a voice in the school curriculum for fear that they will demand snap courses like studies of comic books, TV shows, rock bands, or motorcycle maintenance.

On the other hand, some educationalists believe that there would be fewer drop-outs if at least one or two half-hour courses a week related in some way to special student interests. Such courses could include money-making skills, ways to get along with people, driving courses, and job prospects. As electives, these might also appeal to academic achievers who wish to broaden their curriculum.

The California Board of Education provides high school equivalency exams that test such practical skills as the ability to balance a checkbook and fill out a job application properly. Many teen-agers may want but seldom are able to get that kind of practical knowledge. Some high school students take the equivalency exam, pass it, and get their diplomas without finishing school, where most subjects don't interest or make sense to them and they get poor grades.

A few bright students take the exam early to get their diplomas, then feel free to choose the subjects they will study for the rest of their high school days.

Because most schools offer a program designed for average learners, bright youngsters are often bored. "To work at a normal 'C' student rate is deadly for them," declared Dr. Lewis Keizer, head of a private school for gifted children. "The brighter they are, the more quickly they come to hate school. . . . These kids are our greatest natural resource, yet we do nothing to encourage their talent." Some high schools, recognizing this problem, do provide special work in depth for the brightest teen-agers.

A Harris poll found that 63 percent of students questioned wanted more say in deciding the curriculum. Only 24 percent of parents and 40 percent of teachers, however, agreed that they should have it. Among the subjects students wanted to discuss in class were the use of drugs (70 percent); sex hygiene (52 percent); black students' rights (52 percent); underground newspapers and films (40 percent); hair, dress, and styles (37 percent); and folk rock music (35 percent). Not surprisingly, the most popular topics concerned information that is widely suppressed or misrepresented by adult society as a whole.

Students in the Harris poll defined bad teachers as those

who didn't listen to pupils or let them express opinions, lectured too much, went by the book, lacked a sense of humor, felt they knew it all, and were too strict and impersonal. They also disliked teaching by films or closed-circuit TV because it kept them in a passive role and inhibited questions.

Good teachers were defined as those who were young, had a sense of humor, were willing to listen, didn't follow the book slavishly, encouraged discussion, treated students as grownups, gave them responsibility, were free and open with them, and thought pretty much as they did.

"The key to what is going on among high school students today," Harris reported, "is that a majority clearly want to participate more in deciding their future. They are willing to be taught, but not to be told. They are willing to abide by rules, but they will not abide by rules which put them down. They are aware of the need for authority, but not impressed by it for its own sake. They are excited by the prospect of living in a fast-changing modern society and they want their high school education to help prepare them for it—not for some society of the past."

One seventeen-year-old Marin County, California, girl put it this way: "We need inspiring teachers, not indifferent ones who just give assignments and grade papers. Tenure may be good for teachers, but it's not so good for students when poor or lazy teachers can't be fired. Our junior class wanted to put out a rating book on teachers to help students in selecting electives. The school wouldn't let us do it, even though lots of colleges permit it."

Another frequent criticism of high schools is that many place far greater emphasis on team sports and winning teams than they do on academic achievement. Educationalists question the wisdom of encouraging the lionization of school athletes and assigning passive spectator roles to most of the student body. Athletic coaches have also been accused of exploiting student "jocks" to impress parents with a record of team wins.

Coaches and their defenders argue that high school athletics develops school spirit, teaches teamwork to the players, provides an opportunity for students to yell and ventilate pent-up emotions, and gives them needed relief from the monotony of daily schoolwork.

It is certainly true that many students are more interested in the sports and social aspects of high school than in its academic courses. Often the school accomplishments most highly esteemed by students are those that have little relevance to their own future lives.

As sociologist Lloyd Temme of the Bureau of Social Research in Washington, D.C., observed, "Adolescent social systems reward with prestige achievements that bear little relation to those expected . . . later in life." He added, "As a result, adolescents are ill-equipped to deal with their entry into adulthood, and tend to fall back on their high school achievements as an important part of their lives."

The frustration and rejection many teen-agers encounter in high school at the hands of their more successful peers may leave them with a persistent psychic trauma. In some cases a teen-ager remains consumed with a burning desire to "show them."

The gifted and successful comedian and film director Mel Brooks, who was cold-shouldered in his high school by its athletic heroes, declared, "Thank God for the athletes and their rejection. Without them there would have been no emotional need and . . . I'd be a crackerjack salesman in the garment district."

Superstar rock singer Janis Joplin, who died of a heroin overdose, never forgot or forgave her torturous high school days in Port Arthur, Texas. "In high school, do you know they once threw things at me in the hall?" she said bitterly. "I don't know why. I was strange, sure. . . . They hurt me in Port Arthur." On her death, *Rolling Stone* magazine commented: "She was driven to self-destruction . . . from the moment she left that Texas high school where they had laughed at her. She showed them, all right, she showed them plenty and the dues she paid to show them proved too much in the end."

In his book, *Is There Life after High School?*, Ralph Keyes makes the point that our classmates in high school may play almost as important a role in shaping our lives as our parents.

"The high school imprint," he wrote, "shapes American

adults in such diverse ways—shapes our tastes, our feelings about ourselves in a crowd, and feelings about our bodies."

The women's liberation movement has compelled many states today to bar sex discrimination in the assignment of classes and admission to school activities. Thus, girls as well as boys now have a right to take workshop courses, and boys as well as girls have a right to take homemaking classes.

If pressed, a school board must give the same support to girls' athletic teams as it gives to boys' teams. Some schools have been forced to permit girls who qualify to compete for places on varsity baseball, basketball, and football teams.

A new day is also dawning for another important group of students who have been discriminated against in the past: the almost 4 million handicapped youngsters. Previously, most were refused permission to attend regular schools if they had a physical or mental disability that a teacher or principal judged to be "inimical to the welfare of other students." Over bitter protests from many of their parents, deaf, dumb, blind, retarded, and semiparalyzed children were given a segregated education.

If you're a disabled youngster, a new Federal Education for All Handicapped Children Act now assures you of access to regular schools and, if possible, to the same classes as nonhandicapped children.

A fourteen-year-old Massachusetts boy is a case in point. Paralyzed from the waist down since birth and largely confined to a wheelchair, he was originally refused enrollment in a public school. Admitted at last to a public high school, he did very well. "He's extremely pleased," his mother reported. "He is able to be with kids from the neighborhood, and his social world has expanded."

"The handicapped have to live in the real world," says Tom Poppelreiter, director of special education projects in Scottsdale, Arizona. "If you don't teach them how to live in that world, you are handicapping them even more."

In 1977, Memphis reported 680 assaults in classrooms, 144 of them directed against teachers. In Dade County, Florida, there were 1,153 assaults. In Boston schools, there were 155 assaults on teachers alone. New York City schools reported 2,420 attacks, half directed against teachers. In Chicago schools, five to six classroom attacks a day were reported.

In most states, schools have the right to suspend or expel students who commit acts of violence. Other offenses that schools are not expected to tolerate include threats to a teacher, the possession of dangerous weapons, the use or transfer of drugs, obscene acts or profane language, disruption of classes, and the defiance of teachers or supervisory personnel.

Courts have ruled, however, that schools must have solid evidence to justify any decision to expel any student. The student has a right to examine that evidence and to reply to the charges. Today, about 95 percent of all school expulsions are for smoking marijuana or simply passing a joint to someone else.

The California Board of Education, whose policies are watched and studied by many states, has laid down two requirements for expelling a student: other methods of correction must first have been tried without success, and permitting the student to remain in school must present a continuous danger to the physical safety of the student or to others in the school.

In enforcing discipline, some schools may violate the rights of students. In March 1978, the New York Civil Liberties Union filed suit in federal court on behalf of students who were compelled to submit to illegal searches. One fifteen-year-old Queens girl was forced to strip in the dean's office in a fruitless search for marijuana. School Chancellor Irving Anker acknowledged that this act "went beyond what a school should do."

New York City Board of Education president Stephen Aiello then decreed that all school officials must comply with the Fourth Amendment, which prohibits searches without warrants.

Some high schools seek to curb the student use of cars. One Texas school board ruled that cars taken to school must be parked in the school lot and not used again until school was dismissed. A Texas high-schooler was suspended for driving her car home for lunch. Her parents sued, arguing that the school could not forbid the use of city streets. But an appeals court upheld the school because student cars driven around the school could endanger student pedestrians.

The American Civil Liberties Union upholds the right of high school students to organize groups within the school for any political, social, athletic, or other lawful purpose, provided no student is excluded for reasons of race, religion, or nationality. An Ohio school board sought to discourage such groups by ruling that any member who joined one would be barred from any other school organization.

The school board was sued on behalf of one such group, on grounds that their members had a right to after-school activities and that they could not be kept out of tax-supported school organizations. But the court upheld the school on grounds that private groups tended to undermine good order, discipline, scholarship, and school unity and should be discouraged.

One area in which schools have not been allowed to control student activities is religion. Court decisions have consistently outlawed every attempt by public schools to compel prayer in the classroom, Bible recitations, religious studies, observance of religious holidays, and any other practice that could be considered a violation of the First Amendment requirement of separation of church and state. Students have also won most cases in which their religion or beliefs supported their refusal to salute the flag or to recite the Pledge of Allegiance.

In 1969, the Supreme Court delivered a landmark decision, *Tinker v. Des Moines Community School District*, which compelled school boards to pay more attention to student rights. "School officials do not possess absolute authority over their students," the Court said. "Students in school as well as out of school are 'persons' under our Constitution. They are possessed of fundamental rights which the State must respect, just as they themselves must respect their obligations to the State.... They may not be confined to the expression of those sentiments that are officially approved ... students are entitled to freedom of expression of their views."

In 1976, the Court also specifically declared (*Planned Par-

enthood v. *Danforth*), "Minors, as well as adults, are protected by the Constitution and possess Constitutional Rights."

Thus, you have the right to express your own opinion, whether you agree with your teacher or not, provided you don't disrupt the class. Similarly, you may write and publish or circulate criticism of your teacher, the principal, and the school board, subject to the same laws of libel as adults.

You can read books, whether approved by the school or not. You have the right to meet with friends, when and where you like, provided such gatherings do not violate specific school rules. You may gather with other students before or after school to protest peacefully against anything you don't like and to demonstrate for changes in school regulations or in government policy, if that is your target.

You have these and other constitutional rights *theoretically*, at least. Unfortunately, many state courts differ on the extent to which you can enforce them. Students who have challenged school rulings violating these rights have been upheld in some states, while in others the verdicts in identical cases have gone against them. Very few students or their families have the funds to appeal lost verdicts all the way up to the Supreme Court.

It is, nevertheless, worthwhile to know what your constitutional rights are as they pertain to your school. The school has a legal obligation to inform you of them, with assurances that no punitive action of any kind will be permitted against you if you seek to enforce those rights. Such information can be made available to you through articles in school papers or by distribution of copies of school policy.

If your constitutional rights are violated, simply calling them to the attention of school authorities, along with the verdicts of the Supreme Court in the *Tinker* and *Planned Parenthood* cases, may be sufficient to persuade them to review your case. Often your family lawyer can get effective action for you since his or her presence in the controversy suggests the alarming prospect of a lawsuit.

At the same time, it is important to recognize that your

rights under the Constitution stop where the rights of other students begin. You cannot, for example, interfere with their right to an education in pursuit of some right of your own.

The U.S. Supreme Court has ruled consistently in favor of the right of schools to maintain order by disciplining students who are unruly, disruptive, or violent, including even the right to paddle such students.

But it behooves school principals, who often administer such paddlings, to do so with care. One principal of a junior high school in Alabama was shot twice by an upset thirteen-year-old student he had paddled for disrupting a classroom.

In Florida a principal paddled seventy-one students when someone scrawled an obscene word on a freshly painted bathroom door and no one would tell who had done it. The protests of angry parents forced the removal of the principal by the county school superintendent, who declared, "We can't support mass punishment. This was very poor judgment."

Schools that attempt to operate like educational prisons and students who try to get away with acting like thugs are both operating on the wrong side of the law.

Some school boards, in an effort to achieve a middle-of-the-road approach, are studying the possibility of appointing an ombudsman, an independent official with whom the students could discuss any grievances against school authorities in confidence and who would act promptly to bring about the correction of justified complaints. In high schools, such a person would probably be a teacher liked and trusted by students as "on their side."

The educational process would probably be chaotic if your school did not have the legal power to lay down regulations for the orderly and systematic conduct of classes. But more and more educationalists are coming to the conclusion that you are also entitled to an important voice in the curriculum you are required to study and in school policies.

If you're allowed to give such input, the chances are that you're less likely to drop out.

YOUR RIGHT TO LOOK AS YOU PLEASE

Sharon Ann, a senior in a New York State high school, had been ill, and when she returned to school, the temperature had dropped to just above zero. She had to walk almost a mile to school, and when changing classes, she had to go outside to other buildings. Her mother therefore insisted that she wear slacks to school, despite the principal's rule that girls must wear dresses.

When Sharon showed up in slacks, the principal suspended her from classes. She would not be readmitted, he warned, until she returned clad "properly." The school board upheld his ruling. Sharon's parents appealed to the New York State commissioner of education.

He ordered the school board to reconsider the case. A school district could make *reasonable* rules for student appearance in school, he declared, but a principal's prejudice about not liking to see girls in slacks, which were worn by millions of women, was not reasonable. The school board reluctantly readmitted Sharon in her slacks.

That was in 1966. No girl student today would even think twice about wearing slacks to school.

In earlier times, this right was never very much of an issue. Teens usually followed the style of dress and grooming of adults, often seeking to imitate the avant-garde of adults who led the way in changing styles.

Subsequently, teen-agers sought to initiate their own fashions in dress and grooming to set themselves apart from adults. In many cases these changes reflected the rebellious feelings of young people of the day. For example, during the late nineteenth and early twentieth centuries, Chinese students began a revolutionary movement to reject old ways and modernize China under a republic. Breaking away from traditional dress, they adopted Western-style clothes. Many also cut off their queues, which were considered a sign of obedience to the Manchu throne.

In the United States, following World War I, the 1920s ushered in drastic changes in dress and hair styles that signified a cultural revolution against the last vestiges of the Victorian era.

Young women became "flappers" who bound and flattened their breasts, wore short skirts, and bobbed their hair. Young men wore fur coats and wide-cuffed pants. They aimed for a "modern" look and danced to jazz music.

During World War II, Chicano and black teen-age boys adopted extreme dress and hair styles as a uniform of ethnic defiance. Zoot suits, long pocket chains, and ducktail haircuts distinguished "cool cats" from "Anglo squares." Bad blood between "zoot-suiters" and servicemen led to race riots.

In the 1950s, the "beat generation" revolted against the nuclear establishment and its corporate values. Beatnik men wore black turtlenecks, blue jeans, and sandals and grew unkempt long beards and long hair. Beatnik women wore loose, nondescript dresses or tunics over black leotards. Both used their appearance to make a statement—basically that they had more important concerns than physical appearance on which to spend their time, effort, and money. For some, those concerns were political, artistic, religious, or philosophical; for others, a rejection of middle-class life for a freer, more loving life style.

In the 1960s, black youths seeking a proud African identity wore Afro hairdos and dashikis. White boys and girls dressed alike in blue jeans, sneakers, and shirts hanging out.

In the late 1960s and early 1970s, the revolution in youthful dress and grooming became identified with defiance of the government over the Vietnam War. Conservative police "hassled" unconventionally dressed and groomed teens. A Broadway musical, *Hair*, satirized the conflict between teens and parents over the right to wear long hair and beards.

One landmark case of student grooming was decided in 1970, after Thomas Breen and James Anton were suspended from their high school in Williams Bay, Wisconsin. Their "crime" was having long hair, which, the school maintained, "constitutes a disruption in the school and warrants expulsion."

The American Civil Liberties Union argued the case before a U.S. district court. Federal Judge James E. Doyle ruled that high school bans on long hair were unconstitutional, violating a student's Fourteenth Amendment right to due process of law. Breen and Anton were ordered reinstated, with all mention of their suspension stricken from their school records.

"Education is too important to be granted or denied on the basis of standards of personal appearance," the ACLU insisted. "As long as a student's appearance does not, *in fact*, disrupt the educational process . . . it should be no concern of the school. Dress and personal adornment are forms of self-expression; the freedom of personal preference should be guaranteed along with other liberties."

In a separate California ruling upholding this view, superior court Judge W. G. Watson declared in 1966, "Great care should be exercised insuring that what are mere personal preferences of one are not forced upon another for mere convenience since absolute uniformity among our citizens should be our last desire."

New, unconventional modes eventually influenced the adult world. In sophisticated cities like New York, Boston, and San

Francisco, many adults began to imitate the dress and grooming of teens in an effort to look youthful and "with it." Now many Americans, young and old, dress and groom casually in whatever manner they feel looks and suits them best.

State boards of education, however, have sought to keep the teen-age revolution in dress and grooming within bounds at school. Federal courts usually uphold the school district's right to develop a dress code and specify acceptable hair length.

"A pupil who goes to school without proper attention having been given to personal cleanliness or neatness of dress may be sent home to be properly prepared for school," declares the California code, "or shall be required to prepare himself [or herself] for the schoolroom before entering."

Some school districts have attempted to hold the line on dress and grooming to the extent of curbing more extreme styles. But for the most part adults are resigned to the fact that teenagers today prize their individuality and insist upon dressing and grooming to express it.

Some adults criticize blue-jeaned, T-shirted teens for wearing just as much of a "uniform" as they would be by slavishly conforming to conventional adult dress. "Isn't following the way other teens dress having your life controlled just as much as you think parents control it?" one mother asked her sixteen-year-old daughter. "If doing your own thing is so important, why don't you wear anything at all that takes your fancy, regardless of what other girls are wearing?"

It is true that, for fear of being isolated, many young people, like many adults, dread being different from their peers. Often, for the sake of belonging, they will go against their own principles to join a group that has different standards.

"During high school we don't just *want* the company and good opinion of our peers," declared Ralph Keyes in *Is There Life after High School?*, "we crave it, we need it—we're desperate for their regard as a source of emotional survival."

Research studies indicate that teens who are heavily oriented toward their peer groups tend to be less sure of themselves and to think less of themselves than teens more involved with their families. "What children look for in their friends in such cases," note Dr. Julius Segal and Herbert Yahraes in *A Child's Journey*, "is often what they have failed to find at home."

Thus, if you're exercising your right to look as *you* please—not just as your friends please—you're likely to be in firm command of that area of your life and feeling good about yourself.

YOUR RIGHT TO READ, SEE, AND HEAR WHAT YOU LIKE

In 1977, a girl student at a Massachusetts high school took home an anthology called *Male and Female under 18* from the school library. One of her parents, looking through it, was shocked by a poem written by a fifteen-year-old girl called "The City to a Young Girl." The poem expressed its author's resentment of males who treated her as a sex object.

The parent complained to the publisher of the local paper, who was also chairman of the school committee. He, in turn, found the poem "objectionable, salacious, and obscene." In an article published in his paper, he condemned the book and the school librarian for putting it on her shelves.

At his insistence, the school committee voted to ban the anthology. This action provoked the formation of a Right to Read Committee, composed of two librarians, two teachers, three girl students, and one parent. They filed a class action suit to have the book replaced in the school library.

In court, the students testified that they found the sentiment expressed in the controversial poem to be "realistic and courageous." College professors of literature appeared as witnesses to defend the right of students to read the book.

The court ruled that the school committee had no constitutional right to censor materials selected for school use by the school librarian, administrators, and faculty.

Through the ages, most children's books have been written and published by adults who have decided what young people *ought* to read and like. Most were deadly dull, with the notable exception of fairy tales. Some parents opposed them, too, as filled with violence and encouraging wishful thinking. Others, like Danish immigrant Jacob A. Riis, thought they were fine for children.

"Speaking of Hans Christian Andersen," he wrote in his well-known book *The Making of an American*, "we boys loved him as a matter of course; for had he not told us all the beautiful stories that made the whole background of our lives? . . . I hear of people nowadays who think it is not proper to tell children fairystories. I am sorry for those children. I wonder what they will give them instead. Algebra, perhaps. Nice lot of counting machines we shall have running the century that is to come!"

During the nineteenth century, most American books for children were British reprints, many of them highly moralistic. American writers imitated them, seeking the approval of parents and librarians. The interests of children were secondary.

One prime example was *Little Lord Fauntleroy*, a novel by Frances Hodgson Burnett about an oversweet, sunny little boy who had golden hair in long curls and was dressed in a black velvet suit with short pants and a broad white collar. Thousands of unfortunate little American boys, dressed by their doting mothers as Fauntleroys, had to endure the jeers of merciless playmates.

One American author who was popular with many children was Mark Twain. *The Adventures of Tom Sawyer*, put

1876, enthralled young and old alike with its story of boyhood adventure in a town on the Mississippi. Twain's sequel, *The Adventures of Huckleberry Finn* (1884), was equally popular. People loved both characters because they were portrayed as real children with recognizable emotions, weaknesses, and impulses.

A popular children's book from abroad was Carlo Collodi's *Pinocchio* (1883), adapted from a medieval peasant fable about a puppet who wanted to be a little boy but was led astray by bad companions. Parents thoroughly approved of *Pinocchio* because he taught that lying was bad and that a child's only real safety lay in his home.

Even more to the liking of many children were tawdry paperback novels, which began appearing in 1860 with the publication of *Seth Jones, or the Captives of the Frontier*. These dime novels were melodramatic tales of noble heroes and dastardly villains, read by many adults as well as children, who thrilled vicariously to the improbable tales of high adventure.

Public and school librarians ignored the dime novels, and teachers confiscated those brought into class and read behind open textbooks. Ironically, these trashy paperbacks did more for literacy than the usual dull hardcover books for children, which often gathered dust. Youngsters who devoured dime novels became voracious readers. Many eventually tired of the simplicities of the paperbacks and went on to read more worthwhile books.

The dime novels had an important impact on the thinking and character development of children. Within their framework of exciting melodrama, they were highly moralistic. They stressed the virtues of self-reliance and rugged individualism and the invincibility of plain, honest people in struggles with powerful and evil people.

When competition between dime novel publishers grew intense, some put out sensational paperbacks filled with crime, violence, sin, and sadism. Newspapers, teachers, judges, ministers, and police chiefs denounced them for inspiring lawless behavior.

Before the turn of the century, a more direct appeal to children came in a series of Frank Merriwell dime novels by Burt L. Merriwell was presented as the teen-ager all children dreamed of being. He triumphed over evildoers by sheer nobility of character, courage, and intelligence. New Merriwell paperbacks sold out as fast as they were published.

Another pocketbook series by Horatio Alger, Jr., was aimed at working-class children. Alger heroes in such novels as *Do or Die* were newsboys or other child workers who rose from poverty to successful places in the business world. Alger's first hero, Ragged Dick (*Or Street Life in New York*), remained scrupulously honest despite the temptations of the wicked city. He started up the ladder of success by being rewarded for saving a rich man's son from drowning.

This typical Alger formula, repeated over and over in his novels, led millions of children to fantasize that their determination and noble behavior would be crowned by financial success. Some who did make it up the ladder to fame and fortune gave credit to the Alger books for inspiring them.

In hardcovers, children's love of adventure was appealed to by a Rover Boys series. Youthful fascination with scientific discoveries of the day was capitalized on by a series featuring boy scientist Tom Swift. Girls were offered books like the Bobbsey Twins and Campfire Girls series. Edgar Rice Burroughs's creation Tarzan was also tremendously popular. All these books provided unrealistic heroes and improbable triumphs of good over evil.

Then a few publishers brought out comic books adapted from the comic strips millions of children read daily and on Sundays in the nation's newspapers.

At first the comic books were limited to humor, but as the more mercenary publishers realized that the best-selling comics featured violence, many "funnies" gave way to luridly drawn stories of crime, horror, war and fantasy featuring violence.

These comic books brought vicarious excitement into the lives of many children bored by school and their after-school lives. Millions of youngsters, becoming hooked on violent comics, grew conditioned to pictures as reading material. From 1937 to 1947, there were nineteen different crime comic series. During 1948, over a hundred new titles appeared, with total estimated monthly sales of 80 million. From 1949 to 1954, the vast majority of comics sold featured crime and violence.

Many child experts reacted to this deluge with alarm. Dr. Fredric Wertham, a noted New York psychiatrist, led the attack on lurid comics for having a pernicious effect on the minds and behavior of children. He blamed these comics for encouraging juvenile delinquency and promoting violent conduct. "What they do to children," Dr. Wertham declared, "is that they make them confuse violence with strength, sadism with sex, low necklines with femininity, racial prejudice with patriotism, and crime with heroism.... In this orchestra of violence the comic-book industry has set the tone and the rhythm."

He proposed a law forbidding the display and sale of crime comic books to children under fifteen. Los Angeles County passed such a law, raising the age to eighteen, but the ordinance was declared unconstitutional by the courts. Some twenty-seven other bills seeking similar goals in other states were dropped.

As regular hardcover and paperback books gradually grew more outspoken about sex and freely used street language, many parents became upset when they were made available to adolescents in school and public libraries. In the late 1950s, J. D. Salinger wrote a novel called *The Catcher in the Rye*, whose teen-age hero, Holden Caulfield, stirred empathy among adolescent readers. Because of some sexual content and language, parents pressured many school boards into censoring the book.

Battle lines were formed between, on the one hand, adults and school authorities who considered such books unsuitable for young people and, on the other, adults and teen-agers who felt that teens had every right to read honest, well-respected books like *Catcher in the Rye*. Censorship won out in some school districts but lost in others.

Some ultraconservative parents also sought to censor textbooks and other books available to the young that they considered "subversive" because the authors did not espouse their own ultraconservative political views. In 1962, an organization called Texans for America succeeded in getting that state's Education

Agency to alter every textbook adopted for use in Texas schools. Some fifty books were also removed from the shelves of school libraries.

Defending such censorship, former Texas Congressman Bruce Alger wrote in 1971, "Parents and leaders must look into the whole schoolbook problem from kindergarten through college and ask, 'How did these books get here?' 'Who selected them?' 'Why?' 'Who pays to pollute the minds of young people—whether it is in politics, morals, or economics?'"

In 1977, New York State passed a law threatening prison for up to seven years for anyone "promoting a sexual performance by a child." Many New York booksellers then refused to display or sell a book called *Show Me! A Picture Book of Sex for Children and Parents*. The publisher sued to invalidate the law.

U.S. District Court Judge Robert J. Ward granted an injunction against enforcing it. The book, he said, was "not obscene but a serious, artistic, educational, and scientific book." As such it could not be suppressed. Attempts to censor the book also failed in Massachusetts, Oklahoma, and New Hampshire.

The right of access by you as a teen-ager to books giving sex information is hotly disputed in many parts of the country. Some parents want their children to grow up free from what they consider the troubling aspects of life as far as possible and for as long as possible. "I want my young daughter to be happy," one mother said. "I don't want her made anxious by learning about sex and violence. The only books I want her to read are those which delight her and make her a happier child." Some parents fear books containing sex information will lead children into premature sexual experimentation. Others feel such information should be imparted by parents themselves who can go into the moral considerations that should be part of any discussion of the subject. Others consider information about sex essential to help children understand their sexuality and develop wholesome attitudes toward it. Still others view sex information as vital to help young people avoid unwanted pregnancies and venereal disease.

In seeking to monitor what they consider unsuitable reading material for children, some parents and educators feel that for everything there is a season and that children and young adults are not yet ready for fiction that either glamorizes violence and extramarital sex or presents sex in such explicit detail as to almost be the psychological equivalent for a young person of an actual physical sexual experience. They also object to books that would leave young people with a nihilistic attitude toward life, and they agree with Samuel Johnson's stern dictum: "A book should help us either to enjoy life or to endure it."

Certain other parents and educators, while sympathizing with young people chafing under adult control of their reading material, question whether anyone, child or adult, has an absolute right to read anything and everything. They point out that, just as an individual who enjoys junk food cannot, for reasons of health, stuff himself on it, he likewise has a responsibility to choose his own reading matter wisely and voluntarily to turn away from books that fill the imagination with degrading images or blunt the sensibilities that make us truly human.

Other parents and educators take the position that any unsavory reading material must be tolerated as the price of a free press and argue that "no book ever ruined a child."

Many child specialists tend to step warily between the conflicting positions. At the Child and Family Counseling Center, Santa Cruz, California, psychiatric technician Patrick Graham is concerned about the disturbed children he sees who are exposed to reading material and TV featuring violence and to films like *Jaws* and *Chain Saw Murders*.

"One extremely anxious eleven-year-old kid," he told me, "brought along a highway patrol magazine containing photos of accidents with multilated bodies. He showed me the photos in an obvious state of agitation. I told his mother that she should not let her youngster see such frightening things."

He went on, "I get fed up, however, with parents who say, 'You people out there need to make it easier for me to do my job as a parent.' One woman wrote a newspaper how terrible TV was about sex and violence, and how censorship was needed. But another woman answered, 'You have a hand at the end of your arm; all you need do is turn the TV off.'"

Many parents and educators today feel that for the new "TV generation," reading matter is no longer the major problem. Children, including teen-agers, spend a minimum of three to four hours a day before the TV set. One report on children's viewing estimated that by the time American students graduate from high school, they have spent 10,800 hours in the classroom but at least 15,000 hours watching TV.

The content of much of what young people watch has led disturbed parents to raise questions: What is the effect on small children of watching a program in which parents constantly fight and the father walks out on his wife and child? On pre-teens and teens who watch situation comedies and dramas dealing with extramarital sex, unwed pregnancy, abortion, drug addiction, and alcoholism? On impressionable youngsters who watch factual or fictional scenes of bloody murders, massacres, or war casualties?

TV films depicting violent crimes are accused of inspiring imitation by small children and teen-agers. One mother unsuccessfully sued NBC for over a million dollars for showing a film in which a teen-age girl was sexually assaulted by other teen-agers. Young girls who had seen that film subsequently committed a similar assault upon her young daughter.

Television violence may be troublesome, but it's protected by the First Amendment, a federal judge has ruled in dismissing a Florida suit brought by sixteen-year-old Ronny Zamora and his parents against ABC, CBS, and NBC in 1978, claiming that TV programming "showed the impressionable teen-ager . . . how to kill." Zamora was convicted a year earlier of murdering an eighty-three-year-old neighbor, despite his claim of "television intoxication" caused by viewing such violent shows as *Kojak* and *Police Woman*.

Some parents, nevertheless, charge that much TV programming presents upsetting material that communicates itself so quickly and powerfully to the viewer that a much more vivid impression is left on children than reading about the same thing could create.

A struggle ensued between adults who demanded that programs dealing with sex and violence be kept off TV until late hours when small children were in bed and adults who insisted that such censorship infringed upon their own right to adult entertainment. The Federal Communications Commission tried to compromise by establishing 7:00 to 8:00 P.M. as a "family hour," during which no programs with sex or violence could be shown.

Regular programming for children by all networks has been allocated to the "Saturday morning ghetto," when children are home. They are offered TV cartoons and other programs that one reviewer described as "candy for the eyes." Apart from several good National Educational Television shows, few stretch the mind or the imagination or inspire young viewers.

Millions of children have been made passive captives of the TV set by advertisers who pay $400 million a year to sell sugar cereals and candy to children between the ages of two and eleven. These youngsters spend more hours in glazed staring at the tube than on homework, athletics, games, reading, or family activities.

Many educators blame the sharp decline in reading and writing abilities on the excessive amount of time all children spend in front of the TV instead of with books. Some psychologists worry that half-hour dramas and situation comedies are also feeding children distorted ideas about life and making them feel that every problem has a glib, quick, easy solution.

Some experts, nevertheless, feel that it is unrealistic to deprive children completely of their right to watch.

"I would not want to make my kid that much different from his peers," says Patrick Graham. "If all the kids are watching a whole TV morning of junk programs, I would say, 'Okay, no big deal. You can watch, too. But I don't want you sitting there for four hours watching eight of them. Pick out the two or three you really want to see.' Usually kids will respond to a reasonable compromise."

The one area of entertainment that young people have managed to control in terms of dictating what they want to hear is popular music. Beginning with the cults for Elvis Presley, the Beatles, and Bob Dylan, the young have spent their pocket money to buy the records and tapes, and flock to the concerts, of their favorites. The music business has responded by emphasizing teen-age preferences, especially rock-'n'-roll, with country music a close second. The hard, loud beat of rock-'n'-roll at music festivals continues to draw huge crowds of teen-agers, including those who are enthusiastic about a raucous 1970s brand of the music called "punk rock."

Radio stations cater to teen-age audiences in the music they play. Most records, tapes, and cassettes are produced for people under eighteen. In the music world, at least, teens are not at the mercy of adults. The songs they demand and get stress romantic love, lost love, sex, drugs, the hypocrisy of society, the loneliness of youth, living one's own life free of restraint.

Parents who want to know more about what their teen-age sons and daughters are thinking and feeling might listen to the records they are buying and the radio stations they tune in.

Although high school newspapers are written and edited by students, they are usually subject to adult censorship—direct or indirect—by a faculty adviser or principal.

In 1972, the principal of one Marin County, California, high school was offended when the seventeen-year-old editor of the school newspaper wrote an editorial criticizing one of his orders. Shown the manuscript by the faculty adviser, he banned its publication and suspended the student for writing it.

The student reported these facts to San Francisco newspapers. The next morning, they broke the story that a high school principal had punished a student editor for exercising her First Amendment rights. And they revealed that a lawyer friend of the student's father was bringing suit against the principal.

The principal, alarmed, quickly offered to reinstate the editor if she agreed to let the matter drop. She did so for fear that a protracted legal battle would cause her to miss too many classes, if not her whole senior year, before the court could decide in her favor.

School censorship, insists the American Civil Liberties Union, "should never be exercised because of disapproval or disagreement with the article in question." In California, the state's education code has since firmly established the right of free expression for student publications, limiting the authority of faculty advisers to censor any content except that which is obscene, libelous, or slanderous or incites students to commit unlawful acts.

The problem in many cases is that students who are censored or repressed by school authorities often do not know their rights. Perhaps in time every school will have a Student Civil Liberties Union to advise students of those rights and to help you secure them whenever adults violate them.

YOUR RIGHT TO LOVE AND BE LOVED

At fourteen, Shirley transferred to a new school, where she met Steve, also fourteen, who had curly red hair and a grin that went straight to her heart. After going steady for three years, they planned to marry. At first their parents said they could wed after graduation. Then Steve's father changed his mind, insisting that Steve finish college first.

Feeling betrayed, Steve and Shirley lost interest in their schoolwork. Her grades slipped badly. When Steve began failing several subjects, his father rebuked him severely.

"I'm gonna quit and take a job," Steve said defiantly.

"Doing what—making love?" His father shook a finger. "I'll tell you what you're going to do, young man. You're going to stop seeing Shirley until you pass those subjects you flunked. And give up that crazy idea of getting married at eighteen. You need a college education, and you're going to get one!"

They ran away together. Steve couldn't find a job, but Shirley got work as a waitress in a busy, hot diner. Steve grew depressed at having to live on her earnings. He began to snap at her, suspicious that everything she said had a hidden reproach. Shirley, returning exhausted every night to their dingy two-room apartment, felt herself betrayed by the change in Steve.

What had happened to their romance?

They quarreled often, then retreated into sullen silences, feeling misunderstood. Both were relieved when Steve's parents finally tracked them down. They agreed to go home and return to school when their parents promised to forgive and forget.

They graduated a year later. Although they were still seeing each other, they sensed that their infatuation had cooled and that they no longer seemed the answer to one another's needs. Parting friends, they set off for different colleges. Each subsequently married someone else.

Historically, marriage for love has been the exception, not the rule. For centuries young people were not allowed to have sweethearts openly. They were married off for economic reasons, including dowries paid to parents, at a time of the parents' choosing. Many were delayed in marrying by parents who did not want to lose their labor at home.

In India today, parents still choose husbands for their daughters. If you were an Indian girl between twelve and eighteen, you would usually be forbidden the company of boys and would stay with your own sex. When you were about sixteen, your father would start looking for a husband for you. After he came to an agreement with a boy's father, they might consult an astrologer to see whether the stars and planets favored the match. Then, if your father was willing to offer enough of a dowry, plans for the marriage would go forward.

The boy and his parents might be invited to dinner at your house. You and he would not dare speak to each other, but his parents might ask you a few questions. The next time you would see the boy would be at the wedding ceremony.

You would be shocked by the privilege American girls and

boys have to select their own mates. Considering this the reason for the high American divorce rate, you would prefer to trust to your parents' wisdom in selecting an appropriate and worthwhile mate for you.

In Arab countries, if you were a young man approaching marriageable age, the choice of your bride would be made by your mother and sisters. When negotiations went well, your father and brothers would call at her family's house bearing gifts. If these were accepted, you and she would be considered engaged. After a year you would sign a marriage contract. Another few months, even a year, might pass before you were allowed to take your bride home.

In relatively few countries of the world are adolescents free to select their own dating partners, date them without chaperones, travel and initiate conversations, and make their own choice of marriage partners.

In the United States, boys eighteen or older have the privilege of marrying without their parents' consent in forty states, girls in forty-six states. Most parents oppose early marriage because it places special burdens on teen-age couples that they are seldom mature enough to bear.

In pioneer days, a youthful husband and wife were often self-sufficient, working together to wrest a home from the wilderness and spending most of their time building, farming, making things, and attending to homestead chores. In today's inflated economy, teen-age couples have not had sufficient education to qualify them for the jobs they need to afford a comfortable home and family life.

As a teen-ager you never feel less in control of your life than when you fall in love and seek to make decisions of which your parents disapprove. At such times, parents often seem unreasonable ogres determined to blight a teen-ager's dream of happiness.

Sometimes your parents may, indeed, be unreasonable about your choice of dating or love partners, as well as about your readiness to date, go steady, or marry. But often their opposition may be well founded.

"I couldn't understand why my parents were so down on Charlie," said one young woman, divorcing after four years. "I thought they were blind not to see in him what I saw in him. Now, after getting to know what he's *really* like, I realize I was the one who was blind. But no one could have convinced me of that four years ago—I was too much in love."

Teen-age marriages show the largest number of divorces, breaking up much sooner, as a rule, than couples who marry in their twenties. At sixteen, Louisa married over her parents' objections. When the marriage broke up eleven months later, Louisa found herself pregnant. Taking drugs, she became a heroin addict.

"I just couldn't handle the responsibilities any more," she told the counselor at a drug rehabilitation center. "I tried to be an adult when I wasn't. I thought everything was going to turn out nice, but it didn't."

Parents are even more disturbed by the increase in premarital sexual activity by teen-agers, particularly girls. Of twenty-one million young Americans aged fifteen to nineteen, about eleven million boys and four million girls are estimated to have had sexual intercourse.

For girls, age is a definite factor. One explanation offered is that the age at which puberty begins for American girls seems to be dropping about six months every decade. Whereas a hundred years ago the average girl reached puberty between fifteen and seventeen, according to Sheri Tepper, director of Rocky Mountain Parenthood, a third of all girls now reach that stage at age eleven. And while millions of girls once married between fourteen and sixteen, today's average bride waits until she's twenty-one.

In 1977, a startling study made in California found that one in nine girls between fifteen and nineteen had become pregnant that year. The national rate was only slightly less disturbing: one teen-age girl in ten. More than half of all single girls who have babies are teen-agers. When they keep their babies, the girls often have to go on welfare to bring them up.

"In that sense," observed researcher Kristin Moore of the

Urban Institute in Washington, D.C., "out-of-wedlock births are really a public problem."

Many parents today would not quarrel with a teen-age girl's right to love and be loved by a boy, provided her love stops short of full sexual expression. But few are willing to concede her the "right" to sleep with a boy before marriage. Most object on moral grounds or on the belief that such a course may have unhappy consequences for her.

Sometimes, when there are unpleasant consequences, a parent may be part of the problem. A California divorcée had three teen-age daughters. When the oldest became pregnant, the boy who was responsible agreed to marry her. But the marriage broke up shortly afterward, and she came home to her mother with her baby.

The second daughter then became pregnant. Refusing, likewise, to give up her baby for adoption, she, too, brought it home with her. Some time later, the youngest daughter ran off with a boy at age fourteen. After a few months she returned home pregnant and seriously malnourished. Her mother, who already had her hands full with two daughters and their babies, appealed in despair to the Planned Parenthood clinic in Santa Cruz.

"What have I done wrong?" she wept. "Why is God punishing me like this?"

"Your first mistake," family counselor Mary Zuccaro replied, "was made when your oldest daughter became pregnant. Right then you should have held a family discussion and said, 'Look, we have a problem here. We're going to support her through her pregnancy and help any way we can. However, if we had it to do over again, I would certainly prefer that it had never happened. I hope you two will learn by your sister's mistake. This isn't going to be any picnic for her.'"

Mary Zuccaro went on, "Instead, by devoting all your attention to your oldest daughter and her baby, you made your middle daughter want her share. What better way to get it than with a baby of her own? Ditto the youngest. You made your daughters feel how great it is to have another baby in the house, how easy it was to continue to have a social life afterward. All of them knew that Mama would take care of them and their babies, no matter what!"

On the other hand, many teens consider it hypocritical of society to single them out for punishment for having sex relations while such conduct by unwed adults is frequently shrugged off. A sexually active girl can be taken to family court on her mother's complaint that she is an "uncontrollable" adolescent or a delinquent. But there is little a teen-age girl can do about a separated or divorced mother who has men sleep over.

If parents disapprove of a sexual affair of a daughter who is under the "legal age of consent," which in most states is eighteen, they can break it up by having the boy arrested on a charge of "statutory rape."

In a 1973 study of teen-age sexuality, sociologist Robert C. Sorenson found that only 36 percent of teen-agers saw eye to eye with their parents on sex. Some 58 percent agreed that "a lot of people are leaving home these days because they are seeking sexual freedom." And 74 percent agreed with the statement, "I wish my parents understood that what I do sexually is pretty tame compared to some of the sexual things that go on today."

Most teens wanted to be able to talk to their parents about sex, but only a small number felt that they could. When one fifteen-year-old girl asked her mother a sexual question, she was asked in turn, suspiciously, "What do you want to know for?"

Sometimes teen-agers who have found they cannot communicate with their parents in this matter have been able to get straight answers and helpful guidance through a church or synagogue from ministers, priests, or rabbis trained in pastoral psychology and counseling and committed to respecting confidences.

Some parents are agonized by the shock of discovering that their teen-age daughter has not remained a virgin. One Arizona couple, seeking to punish a daughter who admitted having a love affair with a soldier, handed her a loaded gun. She was ordered to shoot her dog, a pet she loved dearly. Taking the gun, the anguished girl, to her parents' horror, shot herself.

Because we live in a pluralistic society, not all adults share the same moral outlook. One sex educator declared that some parents ask him not to tell teen-agers that sex before marriage is wrong because they don't think it is. Others will say that young people must not be told that sex before marriage is okay because it isn't. "The best I can do," he said, "is present *all* views and hope that those which make the greatest sense to individual teen-agers will prove helpful."

You may be irked by family rules that prohibit a girl and boy from being alone together in a house when parents are absent. Some parents worry more about gossip than temptation.

"It isn't that I don't trust you," one Denver mother told her sixteen-year-old daughter. "I think you'd hold the line. But it wouldn't be any time before whispers about you would get around. That kind of thing is infuriating, I agree. But it's hard to stop and can do a great deal of damage."

It is prudent for teen-age hostesses and hosts to keep their parties in order. Too often parents return home to find indications of sexual activity. When that happens, it may be a long time before another party is permitted in the home.

Few realistic parents expect to be told everything about your dates. But often, when they're confided in, they can offer valuable support in a threatening situation.

Betty, seventeen, told her father that on her first date with eighteen-year-old Richard he had tried to blackmail her into having sex relations. "If you don't," he had warned, "I'll spread the word that I had you and that you're a pushover."

With Betty's permission, her father went to see Richard's father and told him what had happened. When Richard was called to account, he swore that Betty had misunderstood him.

"Maybe so, Richard," his father said. "But if one word of slander against Betty gets around and it can be traced to you, I can promise you'll wish you were never born!"

By having the courage to resist such blackmail and the good sense to seek her father's help, Betty retained both her self-respect and her reputation.

Sometimes, unfortunately, teen-agers' morals are dictated to them by the crowd they hang out with. A third of teen-agers who have sex relations, according to the Sorenson survey, admit that on one or more occasions they had engaged in sexual activities because their crowd had expected them to.

Girls who have premarital sex relations have often admitted to social workers that they didn't really enjoy the sex but consented just to hang on to a boyfriend. Even when they are sexually gratified, it doesn't thrill them that much.

Many teen-agers, both boys and girls, feel driven into early sex in an effort to prove their masculinity or femininity, counselor Mary Zuccaro told me. "The society they grow up in scorns homosexuals, and kids are deathly afraid of being labeled one. Go into school bathrooms and you'll see this kind of graffiti—'Joanie is a lesbie, Bobby K. is a fag.' Boys will proposition girls by saying, 'If you're not a lesbian, prove it!' The subject is so hush hush that in many schools teachers are not allowed to bring up the issue unless students do.

"Most students are greatly concerned about the issue of homosexuality in their lives," she observes. "I try to reassure them that young people go through periods when they prefer to be with their own sex, or have a crush on an older person of the same sex. I explain that most nevertheless develop heterosexual feelings subsequently. When students write their comments, many say, 'Boy, it's a relief to know I'm normal!'"

Another reason for increased sexual activity before marriage is the erosion of moral standards in a large segment of the population. Teen-agers whose parents have strong religious beliefs and who have passed those beliefs on to them will have moral restraints on which to base their avoidance of premarital sex, while other teen-agers may be left by their parents to make their own decision with few guidelines or none at all.

Some authorities think that the increase in premarital sex is the result of bombardment by films, TV, pop music, ads, and the media with messages that sex is vital and that one proves oneself by having sex. Not surprisingly, teens often feel pressured into premature sexual activity.

Other authorities blame the development of the birth control pill. Many teen-age girls manage to obtain and use supplies of the pills without a prior medical exam and subsequent check-ups. Those who do may be incurring serious risks to their health.

Medical supervision is necessary because the pill can cause dangerous blood clots and aggravate such conditions as heart or kidney disease, asthma, high blood pressure, diabetes, and fibroid tumors of the womb. It may also bring on liver tumors, strokes, or eye trouble.

Along with the development of the pill has gone a sharp decline in the use of male contraceptives, which has resulted in an epidemic spread of VD, especially among teen-agers. The high rates of pregnancy and VD among teen-agers suggest that they underestimate the risks of premarital sex.

Some parents worry more about the possibility of a daughter's unwanted pregnancy than about her sexual activity. "Look, we don't want you to have sex before marriage, or at least before you're twenty-one," one Seattle father told his fifteen-year-old daughter. "But if you decide to do so, your mother and I won't be there to stop it, so we want you to be responsible about it. If you're going to have sex, for goodness' sake get yourself some birth control. And use it properly so that you don't wind up with an unwanted baby."

Some parents may inadvertently push their teen-age daughters into having premarital sex. Take the case of Ellen. At fourteen, she had already fended off several boys who had tried to persuade her. Not wanting to seem childish by admitting that she didn't feel ready for sex, she had used the alibi: "Oh, no, I might get pregnant, and if I did, my mother would kill me and my father would kill you."

Ellen's mother, who had been forced to marry in her early teens because of pregnancy, was determined that the same thing would not happen to Ellen. She obtained birth control pills for her daughter. Soon afterward Ellen began having intercourse with boys she dated and contracted VD.

"The day my mother got me the pills, she took away my excuse," Ellen told the social worker at the VD clinic. "I just didn't know how to say no to a boy without hurting his feelings when I knew we could do it without my getting pregnant."

Ignorance or misunderstanding about the use of birth control methods can cause problems for teen-agers using them. Roy and Clara, both sixteen, were secretly engaged. Clara obtained birth control pills, which Roy kept for her so that her parents wouldn't discover them, giving her one pill a day. When he left for vacation, he took the pills with him. Only half jokingly he told her, "As long as I have them, you can't fool around with some other guy!"

During the week following Roy's departure, Clara found herself pregnant. When Roy returned, she told him. He was furious. "That's what you get for fooling around while I'm gone!" he said bitterly.

He refused to see her any longer. Anguished and baffled as to how she could have become pregnant, Clara went to a Planned Parenthood clinic. There she learned that going off the pill had permitted fertilization of an egg cell as a result of their last intercourse.

But Roy refused to believe Clara or come to the clinic to hear the explanation himself. Ignorance of the birth control method they were using caused them to break up, leaving Clara heartbroken and pregnant.

The flood of unscientific sex information in the media today, often presented luridly, only offers many youngsters more undigested facts to be confused about. One twelve-year-old boy read a magazine piece about rare venereal diseases. Shuddering over gruesome photos of the disfigurement they caused, he became so nervous that his mother had to take him to a doctor. Questioned privately, he revealed intense fear that he would suffer disfigurement because of his sexual *thoughts*.

Some child experts insist that teen-agers are entitled to as much knowledge of sex, with as many services and choices, as adults. It is unrealistic and unfair, they argue, to deny them these rights as long as, like adults, teen-age boys can impregnate girls and teen-age girls can become mothers.

In California, schools are authorized to excuse students from classes to obtain, without the need of parental consent, information on birth control, pregnancy, abortion, or VD. All fifty states permit minors to seek treatment for VD on their own. Any teenager who suspects that he or she may have VD can obtain a free, confidential, and anonymous consultation and help by a free phone call to the national VD Hotline. The number is 800-523-1885, in Pennsylvania, 800-462-4966.

Only six states require schools to teach some form of family life or sex education. Other states encourage such courses but leave the decision to require them up to individual school districts. One survey found that only a third of high schools taught anything about human reproduction, sexuality, contraception, or abortion.

In about half the states, children are permitted access to contraceptives at any age. In some states, doctors are permitted to provide birth control information and prescribe contraceptives to minors without the need of parental consent.

Some parents oppose these laws, believing that sex information is the responsibility of parents, who should know best how much to tell their children, when, and how. The school or state, they argue, has no business interfering in this highly personal side of a student's life, in which moral rules, which the schools do not discuss, also apply. Many parents are opposed on religious grounds to the advocacy, sale, and use of contraceptives and to abortion as a choice for pregnant females. They believe that discussing sex and contraception with young people will only encourage them to become sexually active.

"The epidemic of teen-age pregnancies is nurtured by this kind of education being fed to people," declares Judie Brown of the National Right to Life Committee, which opposes abortion as the murder of unborn children.

Marjory Mecklenburg, president of the American Citizens Concerned for Life, disagrees. "If we are not going to fund abortion," she said, "then we have an obligation in the area of support and prevention."

In seeking greater sexual freedom, if you are an unwed girl who becomes pregnant, you usually end up with less personal freedom. If you decide to keep the baby, as 87 percent of unmarried mothers do today, you may not fully appreciate the extent of the difficulties involved in that decision.

You generally have to drop out of school. If you move out of your home, you have to assume, alone, a grueling twenty-four-hour responsibility for the baby. Even if you are able to subsist at a meager level on welfare, your baby's needs will control your life far more relentlessly than your parents ever did.

You may find it impossible to go to work because four out of five day-care centers refuse children under the age of two. Even if you can find day care, you may discover that you can't find a steady job that pays enough to provide for yourself and the baby. To get support, you may feel driven to marry someone who doesn't appeal to you.

If you're the unwed father, your education may be interrupted by the necessity of working in order to contribute to the support of the child, an eighteen-year obligation. And jobs for the poorly educated tend to be low-paying and dead-end.

Many states uphold the right of teen-age mothers to continue at school when they so choose. But principals, teachers, and counselors often pressure them to leave and restrict their extracurricular activities, to isolate them. Some schools operate separate programs for pregnant students and unwed mothers or offer individual instruction in their homes.

For a school to exclude a married or pregnant student, the ACLU states, there must be "compelling evidence that his or her presence in the classroom or school does, in fact, disrupt or impair the educational process for other students." Otherwise she or he cannot legally be denied the right to participate in all the activities of the school.

The ACLU adds, "If temporary or permanent separation from the school should be warranted, the education provided elsewhere should be . . . equivalent to that of the regular school, so far as is practicable."

Parents who want to help prevent you from getting into sexual difficulties may be more effective if they try two-way discussions instead of one-way orders.

"Kids today are growing up in a very different world, one of accelerated change," points out Mary Zuccaro. "Dad might try describing his own experiences and say, 'That's how it was when I was young. . . . Now you tell me how it is now.' By establishing two-way communication, both can share experiences and analyze the decisions that grew out of their experiences. Things aren't all that different when you come down to decisions about whether or not to have premarital sex, whether or not to use birth control, and what to do if contraception fails."

She adds, "These are the same decisions people have been compelled to make for a long, long time. Forms of birth control may change, and society may become somewhat more liberal about sex and pregnant teens. That can affect decision making to some extent. But, basically, things aren't all that different."

More educational work needs to be done with boys, particularly along the lines of taking responsibility for their sexual experiences. It takes two to make a baby, and both partners are equally responsible for creating a new life.

A popular 1978 movie, *Saturday Night Fever*, impressed millions of teen-agers who saw it when its macho hero, played by John Travolta, was shown halting a sexual liaison with a girl as he realizes that neither of them is prepared with a birth control method. The message was clear: teens who don't want to take on responsibility for a child should either abstain from intercourse or use birth control.

More often than girls realize, boys feel driven to proposition them because they feel it's expected of them as "redblooded" males. Frequently boys, younger teens especially, secretly hope that the girl will say no.

A girl can play the game skillfully if she has "safety lines" which let her refuse gracefully and tactfully. For example: "You know, if there was any person I would ever want to have sex with, it would be you. But I honestly don't feel emotionally ready for it, so I hope we can continue to enjoy each other on other levels."

For many teens who want to love and be loved, there are a lot of important problems to work out with each other before marriage, without complicating them by irresponsible sex.

YOUR RIGHT TO WORK OR NOT TO WORK

Eight-year-old Davey was one of old Chicago's poor children whose parents felt compelled to let him work in a factory operating dangerous machinery. Caught up in a machine, Davey was badly mangled and died in agony. The factory owners had saved money by not equipping the machines with safety guardrails, even though two children had been previously injured.

When Davey's parents sought compensation, the factory manager produced a document they had signed as a condition of Davey's employment. The fine print stated that no claim could be made for any accident resulting from a worker's "carelessness." The owners continued to hire cheap child labor for the perilous work, while still refusing to install guardrails.

Such were the conditions of child labor in the United States in 1889, impelling social-work pioneers like Jane Addams to fight for laws to free children from industrial slavery.

Through the centuries, children had been expected to contribute to the family income, usually by farm work and spinning or weaving cloth. Orphans, especially, were expected to earn their own keep by being hired out. In 1697, the courts of Chester County, Pennsylvania, sold thirty-three orphans into temporary servitude.

Poor children were widely exploited in Europe, especially after the Industrial Revolution required cheap labor in the burgeoning factories. When the first cotton mills sprang up in England at the end of the eighteenth century, the owners sent agents to collect pauper children throughout the kingdom. Their services were obtained for just the price of their maintenance. Children as young as five were compelled to work thirteen to sixteen hours a day at jobs that often ruined their health.

American mill owners were quick to follow suit. In 1798, when one of the first major mills opened in the United States, owner Samuel Slater hired poor children aged seven to twelve.

Alexander Hamilton saw nothing wrong in this system, since he himself had had to go to work at the age of twelve when his merchant father went bankrupt. Thomas Jefferson disagreed. He deplored the factory system, especially its brutal exploitation of small children.

In England, boys and girls as young as five who were sent up chimneys as chimneysweeps contracted skin diseases and lung ailments from the soot. When reformers tried to prevent this use of child labor, the Earl of Lauderdale warned Parliament that if it passed such an act, the wealthy would retaliate by cutting back their contributions to children's charities.

The Religious Tract Society offered a different solution. It urged chimneysweeps to wash well on Saturdays and attend Sunday School. "Thus," it declared, "you will be happy little sweeps." Not for another ninety years did Parliament get around to passing a law prohibiting the use of children in chimneys.

In early nineteenth-century America, many community leaders had a puritanical abhorrence of idleness among children. In 1808, an ad taken in the *Federal Gazette* by a Baltimore cotton mill urged readers with a "knowledge of families who have Children destitute of employ" to "do an act of Public benefit by directing them to this institution." Boys and girls aged five to seven from poor families were kept out of school and crowded into airless factories to work from sunup to sundown as mill hands. The practice was widespread.

Some disturbed legislators protested that children belonged in schools, not factories. In 1811, Connecticut passed a law requiring mill owners to provide lessons in reading, writing, and arithmetic for their child workers. Few states followed suit. A Philadelphia study in 1830 found that only one in six child workers in cotton mills could read or write her or his name.

But by 1836, New England reformers had become influential enough to compel a Massachusetts law to be passed requiring at least three months of schooling a year for every child factory worker under fifteen. Other New England states began limiting the working day for factory children to ten hours.

Many cotton textile manufacturers thereupon began moving south, where state legislatures obligingly refused to place any curbs on the use of cheap child labor.

Across the Atlantic, in 1829, Charles Dickens's father was sent to debtor's prison. Ten-year-old Charles was forced to go to work at difficult, unpleasant labor in a warehouse.

"It is a matter of surprise to me," he wrote later, "that I can have been so easily thrown away at such an age. A child of excellent abilities and strong powers of observation, quick, eager, delicate, and soon hurt bodily or mentally, it seems wonderful to me that nobody should have made any sign in my behalf. But none was made; and I became, at ten years old, a little labouring hind."

English children as young as seven were virtually enslaved in coal mines, as well as in cotton and silk mills. Mine children usually worked from 6:00 A.M. to 5:00 P.M. and were often beaten for not pulling the carts fast enough.

In 1842, a British Factories Inquiry Commission reported to Parliament, "Chained, belted, harnessed like dogs in a go-cart, black, saturated with wet, and more than half-naked—crawling upon their hands and feet, and dragging their heavy loads behind them—[the children] present an appearance indescribably disgusting and unnatural."

In that year, Massachusetts limited the working day of children under twelve to ten hours. Six years later, Pennsylvania prohibited the employment of any child under twelve in a silo or a cotton or wool mill. The use of child labor nevertheless increased vastly with the industrial expansion that followed the Civil War.

Many immigrants sent their children to work because their own jobs did not pay enough to feed the family. Others simply sought to amass as large a family income as possible. They often lied about their children's ages to get around state laws setting a minimum working age. One reformer, John Spargo, deplored "the senseless, feverish, natural ambition of the immigrants to save money, to be rich . . . to barter the manhood of their sons and the womanhood of their daughters for gold."

In 1887, Karl Marx observed caustically, "Now the capitalist system buys children and young persons under age. Previously, the workman sold his own labor-power, which he disposed of nominally as a free agent. Now he sells wife and child. He has become a slave dealer."

In the latter part of the nineteenth century, most farm children either still received no schooling or went to school for the equivalent of three months a year. Up at five to milk cows, they would then feed livestock, pump and carry water, churn butter, and help with the harvest for long hours every day. Because of the power of the farm vote, farm children were usually the last to be protected by child labor legislation.

By the end of the century, almost a fifth of all American children between the ages of ten and fifteen were wage earners. Many were employed at dangerous occupations in factories, mines, and mills. British novelist H. G. Wells, visiting New York City, was appalled by the use of young boys after dark as telegram messengers and newspaper venders. "Nocturnal child employment is a social abomination," he declared. Newsboys were often in peril of beatings. Competition between newspaper publishers was so fierce that some hired thugs to attack rivals' newsboys and drive them off the streets.

In 1904, the National Child Labor Committee (NCLC) was organized to fight child labor practices that were ruining the health or lives of children and depriving them of an education. Young children were still working long hours day and night in coal mines, at white-hot glass-blowing furnaces, in dust-filled cotton mills, in unsanitary factories and tenement sweatshops, in damp canneries, and in street trades.

Quaker poet Sarah Cleghorn grew indignant when she saw a textile mill employing children right next to a beautiful golf course. In her book *Portraits and Protests* (1917), she wrote this stinging indictment of a callous society:

> The golf links lie so near the mill
> That nearly every day
> The laboring children can look out
> And see the men at play.

NCLC investigators found children working under appalling conditions. In Pennsylvania coal mines, young boys were paid sixty cents a day to stoop over dusty coal chutes sorting slate from coal. Many child workers were crippled or badly hurt and sometimes killed in accidents. In one mine that employed thousands of young children, fourteen-year-old Frank had both legs cut off at the knees when run over by a coal car.

Some of the most heart-rending cases were found in New York City, where six- and seven-year-old children worked from dawn until long after dark in canning factories. Many children were employed in small sweatshops or were kept up until late at night stripping tobacco in dim, dingy slum flats.

When not in school, every hour of eleven-year-old Rose Peccaro's time was occupied making artificial flowers for women's hats at three cents a gross. Pasqualina, twelve, got up at 6:00 A.M. to crochet Irish lace for two hours before school, then for three hours afterward, for eighteen cents a day. Work for children in a shirt factory began at 2:00 A.M. and in rush seasons ended at 10:00 P.M., with no time out for meals. Children too exhausted to get up mornings in time for work were beaten by their parents until they did.

NCLC investigators found thousands of "gutter children" like Jack, who left school in the primary grades to shine shoes. "He lives in the gutter—seven days a week—from seven in the morning until eleven or twelve at night," the investigators reported. "He rarely goes home at all. He is thirteen years old; his height is four feet."

In 1916, persistent pressure from the NCLC finally compelled Congress to pass a law forbidding the employment of children under fourteen in nonfarm industries whose products were sold interstate. The law was struck down by the Supreme Court as unconstitutional in a five-to-four split decision. A sarcastic versifier of the day observed:

> Five reverend, wise and gentle men
> Have thrust the babies back again.

A second child labor law passed that year was also declared unconstitutional. Only thirteen states, meanwhile, had their own laws curbing the use of child labor. Big business interests fought tooth and nail against all such laws. Where their lobbies could not prevent passage, they managed to weaken the laws and make them difficult to enforce.

The first real national reform came under Franklin D. Roosevelt's New Deal administration. A minimum age of sixteen was established for workers in most industries and eighteen for hazardous occupations. The Supreme Court once again ruled such laws unconstitutional. The New Deal Congress then passed the Walsh-Healey Act prohibiting firms with federal contracts from employing boys under sixteen and girls under eighteen. The Sugar Act also reduced subsidies to any beet growers who used children under fourteen or worked those fourteen or fifteen longer than an eight-hour day.

In 1938, Congress passed the Fair Labor Standards Act. It banned from interstate commerce all goods made by industries employing children under sixteen, as well as products made in hazardous industries employing youngsters under eighteen. The act, however, did not affect businesses whose products did not travel across state lines; many farms, canneries, laundries, hotels, garages, restaurants, amusement places, and stores fell into this category.

Defense production during World War II brought a large influx of children to take the place of workers who were called to military service. Over a million youngsters between fourteen and fifteen and two million between sixteen and seventeen joined adult workers in defense industries.

After the war, the government initiated a "Back to School" movement, but the Labor Department found that 2.2 million children seventeen and under remained in the work force.

Child labor laws today differ from state to state.

Generally, however, if you are between the ages of twelve and eighteen, you need a work permit to be employed. Exceptions include working for your parents or a farmer or for yourself, as a babysitter, gardener, golf caddy, woodchopper, or the like.

Under twelve, you can also usually work for your parents or deliver newspapers without a permit. As a minor, however, you are not permitted to work in certain hazardous occupations or in bars or liquor stores.

Your parents have the legal right to your earnings until you are eighteen, in return for your food, clothing, shelter, medical care, and educational costs, unless you are paying for these items.

The question of the use of children in farm labor has remained a gray area. For generations, in Oregon and Washington, ten- to twelve-year-olds have earned money picking strawberries with their families, even though the Fair Labor Standards Act originally prohibited such child labor. Congress, under pressure from the farm belt, amended the act to allow children to do such work if the farmer got a waiver from the Department of Labor.

But in 1978, Labor Secretary Ray Marshall spiked the amendment by refusing to issue any waivers. Farmers from both states filed suit against him. They argued that without the 6,000 children who normally help with the harvest and without the mothers who stay home with them, up to 30 percent of the crop wouldn't get picked. The farmers claimed they would lose up to $13 million. A federal judge issued an order temporarily letting the child strawberry pickers back into the fields.

Proponents of your right to work argue that, by forbidding your employment, the government is arbitrarily controlling and curbing your rights. Child labor laws were admittedly necessary to prevent the exploitation of children in the past, they concede, when unscrupulous businessmen robbed them of their childhood. But it is another matter, they insist, when today's young workers have the full protection of the law and wish to work for experience or money. They believe that holding a job is a valuable experience for you, teaching you responsibility and making you aware that there are no "free rides" in our society.

Defenders of the child labor laws nevertheless feel that children have an absolute right to their childhood until they are sufficiently educated and mature to fend for themselves.

In many other parts of the world today, work for children as young as six or seven is simply a way of life. The International Labour Office (ILO) reports that there are now 52 million child workers under fifteen, most of them exploited, some mistreated. About 42 million work without pay in family enterprises, particularly on family farms. About 10 million are wage earners in factories, fields, and workshops.

Child labor is most widespread in South Asia (29 million), East Asia (9 million), and Latin America (3 million). The actual figures are probably larger, because many countries do not report child labor statistics. In others, children who work and also attend school, however briefly, are often not counted.

An ILO survey in an industrial area of Asia found that small, undernourished children, especially girls, constitute a great part of the work force. They labor long hours, seven days a week, for a pittance. Many are employed in overcrowded, poorly lit, and badly ventilated plants that make or pack bottles, cigarettes, textiles, candy, biscuits, and seafood. In some plants, adult workers hire child "helpers," who actually do all the work for a fraction of the adult wages.

If you were such a child hired as an apprentice, you would find your training negligible. Treated like a servant, you would not even be paid enough for your meals. Your task would often be highly dangerous, like operating an acetylene torch, using cutting and piercing tools, and working near furnaces. Throughout most of Asia, Latin America, the Middle East, and southern Europe, you would also be used as a casual laborer on building sites.

In some countries, it would be legal to employ you as a domestic servant. Children as young as seven—mostly girls—are brought into cities from the countryside in Central America, the Middle East, and some parts of Asia. You might be sold into service by poor parents or by adults who have bought or kidnapped you. And abuse of child servants is not uncommon.

Child labor has a long history in countries like Egypt, where 90 percent of all children employed are in agriculture, 7 percent—mostly girl house servants—in domestic service, and 4 percent in industry. From 1937 until today, the number of employed girls under fifteen has increased from less than 12 percent to 36 percent. The Egyptian government estimates that by 1985 they will make up a third of the female labor force.

On the other hand, boys under fifteen make up only 9 percent of the male labor force, and this ratio is not expected to increase. The reason reflects sex differences in school enrollment. In Arab countries, boys are favored over girls.

In Egypt's cities, 37 percent of all children aged six to nineteen are employed. Child labor is even higher in rural areas.

In much of the world, if you had to labor on a family farm, you would get little or no education. Your labor would often make the difference between existence and starvation for your family. You would probably grow up illiterate, doomed to menial, poorly paid work for the rest of your life.

"Any society which wants its children to be free to learn and play," declares Jan Vitek of the International Labour Office, "must first free its entire population from fear of want. This means ensuring basic human needs of all people . . . food, shelter, clothing, water, education, training, and provision of gainful employment."

These goals are obviously a long way off. Meanwhile, the ILO is seeking to get more countries to ratify and implement its resolutions calling for a fifteen-year minimum age for all workers and the protection of working children from exploitation, hazardous working conditions, night work, heavy work, long hours without rest, and the denial of basic education and training.

YOUR RIGHT TO PROTEST AGAINST AUTHORITY

In 1978, on the thirty-third anniversary of the U.S. atomic attack on Hiroshima, antinuclear domonstrations broke out all across the country at nuclear power plants. The demonstrators protested nonviolently, using civil disobedience tactics to disrupt the operation of the plants.

Leaflets were handed out to plant workers warning them of the hazards of radiation. Some demonstrators climbed fences and occupied the plants. Others sat down in front of the main gates to block them. Ordered by police to disperse, they stayed put.

Most refused to cooperate with their arresters and went limp, having to be dragged off. Some stood in circles singing protest songs until they, too, were dragged off. Groups of demonstrators locked arms and had to be pulled apart. Thousands belonging to such antinuclear organizations as the Abalone Alliance and People for a Nuclear-Free Future were jailed. Idealistic teen-agers were among the protesters, exercising their First Amendment rights.

Children have always been considered powerless to correct what they have viewed as unjust in their society. Many have nonetheless felt driven to protest. It is in the nature of children to be passionately idealistic, unlike many adults, who, made cynical by experience, shrug and say, "That's the way the world is, and you can't change it." Many children believe, "That's the way the world shouldn't be, and we want to try to change it."
During the Middle Ages, children tried to change things on a massive scale in the renowned Children's Crusade. By the thirteenth century, four Christian crusades to recapture Jerusalem from the Moslems had failed, and adult knights refused to mount a fifth crusade, calling it suicidal. A twelve-year-old shepherd boy in France, Stephen of Cloyes, believed that Jesus Christ had asked him to lead a crusade of children to win back Jerusalem, not by defeating the Moslems but by converting them.
Preaching to children, Stephen's message inspired thousands and spread to Germany. Children flocked to his banner and that of his German disciple Nicholas. Marching on foot across both countries to set sail for the Middle East, the child crusaders proclaimed themselves more valiant and chivalrous than the adult knights who had rejected the Pope's summons.
The Children's Crusade ended in disaster. Most of the enlistees were lured away and exploited by unscrupulous adults along the line of march and never reached a port of embarkation. Those who did obtain transport to the Middle East were taken there by slavers, who sold them to Moslems. These children remained in slavery for the rest of their lives.
Ill-fated and doomed, the Children's Crusade nevertheless reflected the idealism of youth. Some children undoubtedly ran off to join the crusade for adventure or escape from unhappy home lives, but most were inspired by a sense of high purpose. They saw the rescue of the Holy Land from "infidel" hands as a solemn obligation to their God and civilization.
Many idealistic children also took part in the American Rev-

olution to protest the injustice of British rule. For example, Ebenezer Fletcher, sixteen, who enlisted in 1777 as a fifer in Colonel Nathan Hale's regiment, was wounded in the back in his first battle and taken prisoner. Escaping, he made his way back to his regiment through the wilderness, surviving attacks by wolves and Indians.

Children usually took seriously the ideals taught them in schools and churches. Before the Civil War, they were enlisted by Sunday school teachers to march in temperance parades. The children dramatized the protest against saloons, where some fathers drink away weekly wages, leaving their families in need.

From the 1930s through the 1970s, American youth became increasingly cynical about adults who ran their lives. They were confused and angered when they found society preaching one set of standards but living by another.

Yet during the 1950s, students did not dare openly question or challenge the "Establishment." Called the Silent Generation, they kept quiet while witch hunts raged through the country, repressing dissent by labeling liberals as communists. Those who sought to protest were often painted with the same red brush, blacklisted from jobs, and put under FBI surveillance.

Some disgusted students simply dropped out of the system to join a beatnik counterculture that renounced the standards and goals of middle-class adult society and in particular opposed nuclear weapons. Finding the business world and government too materialistic and hypocritical, beatniks refused to conform. They replaced clean-shaven faces with scraggly beards, crew-cuts with long hair, neat dress with ragged jeans and open shirts, neckties with beads and pendants, conventional beds with mattresses on the floor, drinking with smoking pot, marriage with living together, conversation about baseball, golf, and business with rapping about poetry, sitar music, and oriental mysticism.

In the 1960s, youthful dissent turned more openly political. Young people challenged the older generation's obsession with the Cold War, militarism, and business profits. Teen-age hippies—a later generation of beatniks—crusaded nonviolently for new causes: an end to pollution of the environment for the sake of profit, an end to racial injustice, an end to warmongering. Love and peace became passwords. When troops were called out to intimidate demonstrators, hippie children stuck flowers in their gun barrels.

Fed up with the way most adults in the world were running things, youth movements arose in many other countries as well. Their revolt was directed first at universities, which were viewed as cultural factories serving big business and military research. Students demanded greater control over their own lives, beginning with the universities they attended.

In the United States, France, Germany, Mexico, and other countries, students went out on strike, seizing university buildings, shutting them down, and sometimes causing property damage. There were stormy battles with police sent on campus to arrest them.

This world-wide student revolt shook many university administrations, which subsequently agreed to give students a greater voice in university affairs.

Although radicals participated in, and frequently led, the university revolutions, many moderates also took part.

Brian Turner, nineteen, participated in the 1964 student revolt at Berkeley over the right of students to free speech on campus. When he set up a table to distribute strike literature, he was threatened with expulsion. "I folded up the table and went home," he related. "But I thought about it overnight and I went back. When they came up to see me again, my own principles prevented me from leaving. I had decided that the freedom of 27,000 people to speak freely is worth the sacrifice of my own academic career."

At a rally of 6,000 Berkeley students, strike leader Mario Savio told them, "There's a time when the operation of the machine becomes so odious, makes you so sick at heart, that you've ... got to put your bodies upon the gears and upon the wheels, upon the levers, upon all the apparatus, and you've got to make it stop. And you've got to indicate to the people who run it, to the people who own it, that unless you're free, the machine will be prevented from working at all."

Three years earlier, California Governor Pat Brown had said in a Berkeley commencement address: "I say: thank God for the spectacle of students picketing—even when they are picketing me at Sacramento and I think they are wrong—for students protesting and freedom-riding, for students listening to society's dissidents, for students going out into the fields with our migratory workers, and marching off to jail with our segregated Negroes. At last we're getting somewhere. . . . Let us stand up for our students and be proud of them."

However, at the height of the campus disturbances, Governor Brown ordered the Berkeley strikers arrested. Many students were hurt as 500 police swept onto campus, manhandling girls as well as boys and making 782 arrests.

Outraged by this treatment of students, most of the faculty threw their support behind the strike. The university was virtually shut down; the "machine" was prevented from working. When the strike was finally resolved, many student demands for reform were incorporated into new regulations.

Student revolts flared up during the 1960s and early 1970s over many issues: university cooperation with the Vietnam War, courses that prepared students for jobs that would soon cease to exist, discrimination against women and minorities. Students staged demonstrations, sit-ins, and violent confrontations with police. Sometimes the protests got out of hand and property was damaged. The adult world was startled into paying attention.

The student revolution intensified with the stepping up of the Vietnam War and the draft of large numbers of American youths to fight it. Many draft resisters went to jail for insisting that they had not been consulted about Vietnam and therefore had no obligation to give up their lives to fight what they considered an unjust, brutal war.

Students in Illinois who protested being punished for reading an antiwar underground newspaper, the Washington *Free Press*, were told by their principal, "I don't want to hear anything about constitutional rights, student rights, human rights, or any other rights." Another high school student who sought to participate in an anti-Vietnam protest in front of his school was warned by the vice-principal that if he did, the school would see to it that he would not be able to get into any college.

In one landmark case, *Tinker v. Des Moines Community School District,* Iowa high school students wore black arm bands to classes to signify mourning over the Nixon adminstration's insistence upon prolonging the Vietnam War. Ordered to remove their arm bands, they refused and were suspended. When they took their case to court in 1969, they were upheld in their right to protest the war silently by wearing the arm bands. The court held the arm bands to be symbolic free speech protected by the First Amendment and called children "persons" under the Constitution.

In the late 1960s, when unrest swept from college campuses to junior and senior high schools, students began protesting against everything from arbitrary grading systems to bad cafeteria food. Denied the columns of official school papers, many students began putting out their own underground papers. A 1969 study reported over a thousand of these in existence.

The New York City Board of Education was the first to recognize the constitutional rights of high school students. At the end of 1969, it issued a policy statement acknowledging their rights to have a voice in school matters affecting them, to have school papers largely free of censorship, to express political views through buttons and arm bands, and to distribute political leaflets near the school. The board later specified that student dissent must be nonviolent and must not interfere with classes. Many other boards of education were not that liberal.

In 1971, a White House Conference on Youth upheld "the right of the individual to do her/his own thing so long as it does not interfere with the rights of another," but just which constitutional rights students enjoy is still often a matter left to state courts to decide.

When antiwar demonstrations finally succeeded in ending both the Vietnam War and the draft, the steam went out of the resistance movement. By the time Jimmy Carter was elected President in 1976, few young people were still involved in major protest movements. Some had became attracted to various religious cults that rejected mainstream America. Others had transferred their dissent to environmental concerns.

Factory wastes were increasingly polluting the water young people had to drink, in some cases making it dangerously radioactive. Multiplying nuclear power plants increased the level of background radiation in the environment, threatening genetic changes in the unborn and generating the danger of catastrophic nuclear fall-out in case of accident. More and more of the food young people had to eat was being adulterated with chemical preservatives and other additives suspected of causing cancer. Unscrupulous whaling and tuna fishing industries were killing too many whales and dolphins, making them endangered species. Money-hungry real estate developers were replacing America's dwindling green spaces with shopping malls and mobile-home parks.

A sign that American society was beginning to give a public voice to junior and senior high school students came in 1978 when the *Ladies' Home Journal* published a national survey of the views of 800 of them. In students' eyes, the two adults who had done "the most damage to the world" were Adolf Hitler and Anita Bryant, chief opponent of homosexual rights. The adults who made students angriest were Bryant and ex-President Richard Nixon. The adults considered to have done "the most good for the world" were Abraham Lincoln and Eleanor Roosevelt.

The relative passivity of students in the late 1970s led some adults to compare them to the "Silent Generation" of the 1950s. Dissent was no longer the mood of the day, except for the women's movement and adult backlashes like the taxpayers' revolts.

But the court battles fought in the 1960s and early 1970s established the right of student dissent. The courts held that it is a violation of free speech to require students to say what they do not believe. A student today, for example, may stand quietly during the Pledge of Allegiance or refuse to salute the flag if it is against his or her religious beliefs.

If the spirit of dissent has grown quieter, it has not completely disappeared. When the voters of California passed Howard Jarvis's Proposition 13, slashing property taxes and thus making less money available for schools, one indignant twelve-year-old wrote to his local paper: "We sit around today ... with no summer school or enrichment classes. A question arises among us: Why do us kids not even get a word in about an issue concerning us so as Proposition 13? But, gee whiz, they say. He's only a kid who doesn't know what he's talking about. You would be surprised. ... If people can afford to buy the expensive houses, why can't they afford the expensive taxes? Baloney, say us eighth grade linguists. Us kids are worth more than you think."

YOUR RIGHT TO JUSTICE UNDER THE LAW

The families of 350 New York City children in institutional care were upset when the city, seeking to relieve crowded conditions, transferred them to institutions in other states. Many of the families were too poor to afford the transportation costs for regular visits. On visiting days, children waited in vain for parents.

One sixteen-year-old retarded boy was shipped to Vermont, where his ill mother could not visit him. Believing himself to have been abandoned, the boy fell into a severe depression.

At a Virginia institution to which forty children had been sent, one young girl was alleged to have been raped, another assaulted. A seventeen-year-old complained that he had been harshly manhandled and forced to take powerful drugs. Similar complaints were voiced by ninety children sent to a Florida institution.

The New York Civil Liberties Union filed a class action suit against both New York City and New York State, seeking to compel them to develop local programs for the deported children that would provide supervised treatment near their homes.

Society has frequently taken a callous view of children whose parents were unable to care for or control them, thus burdening taxpayers with the cost of their supervision. There is little public sympathy for young people who balk at the rules society has laid down for them, sometimes apparently just for the sake of rebellion.

This antipathy has a long, ancient tradition. Archeologists unearthed a 3,000-year-old Sumerian tablet, displayed in the University of Pennsylvania museum, preserving this conversation: "Where have you been?" "Nowhere." "If you didn't go anywhere, why must you be loitering? Go to school. . . . When you have finished and reported to the teacher, come to me and don't just walk the streets. Did I make myself clear?" In 1654, the Massachusetts Bay Colony prescribed whipping for children who disobeyed their parents or showed disrespect.

The term "juvenile delinquent" is of relatively recent origin. Before the twentieth century, little distinction was made between children and adults accused of criminal behavior. Boys and girls as young as ten and twelve were imprisoned in vile jails with hardened adult criminals. Some were hanged, lashed, burned at the stake as witches, branded, or sold as indentured servants. In the early nineteenth century, a ten-year-old English boy was hanged for stealing a letter from a mailbox.

During the first half of that century, as impoverished immigrants flocked into American cities, growing slums gave rise to criminal teen-age gangs. Much juvenile delinquency took the form of gang fights and antisocial pranks. One boy's diary recorded a gang fight involving 800 teen-agers, then added: "Stole pigeons. Broke into slot machines. . . . Tie a rope across the street and trip people up. Throw eggs at people. Throw cabbages at people. Ring doorbells. Break windows, electric lights. . . . Plague Jews and Italians. . . . Have a dead rat. Throw it at Chinaman."

At the close of the nineteenth century, upset by the brutal

treatment of children thrown into adult prisons, reformers agitated for special juvenile courts. There, presumably, benevolent judges would take into account the tender age of the accused children and the lack of proper nurture to keep them out of wrong paths. If you were a youngster in trouble, instead of punishing you, such courts were expected to rehabilitate you by removing you from your slum environment. You would be sent to a place in the country where you could be reeducated in wholesome ways. Here you would also be spared the assaults and schooling in crime that followed incarceration in adult jails.

The first juvenile court was established in Cook County, Illinois, in 1899, for "individual treatment through the helping professions." Illinois Judge Julian Mack declared, "The problem for determination by the judge is not, 'Has this boy or girl committed a specific wrong, but What is he; how has he become What he is; and What had best be done in his interest and in the interest of the state to save him from a downward career.' "

But problems quickly developed in what had begun as an enlightened act of idealism. The court at first handled only juveniles from seven to sixteen who committed acts that, when performed by adults, were punishable as crimes. But soon children also began to be brought to juvenile court for offenses that, when committed by adults, were *not* considered crimes—for example, "incorrigible conduct," "truancy," "running away from home," "smoking tobacco," and "using intoxicating liquor." The courts also became a dumping ground for children who had committed no offense at all but were problems for society because of parental neglect or abuse.

In the institutions to which most were sent, runaways and abused and neglected children were often thrown together with dangerous delinquents who had committed serious crimes. "Over half of the youths in Juvenile Center did absolutely nothing but run away from home, including myself," said a seventeen-year-old New Yorker who testified before a Senate committee in 1971. "A person who has family or personal problems should not be put in places like this.... It does no good to tell the counselors you are being bothered or threatened by other girls because they are really unable to provide any real control.... In Juvenile Center you either live or die. When the girls start with their physical violence, there is no way out and no one you can tell. You go to sleep hoping you'll wake up next morning.... I am not here to have any campaign against lesbianism, but I object to its involving me."

She added, "Just about everything you eat is powdered or looks like something that just came out of the garbage. If you have any intelligence, you will die of starvation.... The living conditions in these places are horrifying. You are thrown together like a bunch of animals in a cage. We are human and do not deserve to live like this.... I have heard of youths being sent to youth houses because their parents did not want their children at home and there is no other place for them.... These conditions are for untrained animals, not youths who are having enough trouble with themselves growing up."

Children in some detention centers were whipped on the hands and wrists with key chains, placed in solitary confinement for indefinite periods, and held for up to a year awaiting placement. Conditions were so bad at one training school for girls in New York that it had to be shut down.

Before 1967, if you were brought to juvenile court, you were usually at the mercy of the judge and had none of the rights guaranteed to arrested adults. That situation changed in 1967 with a Supreme Court decision in the case *in re Gault*.

Gerald Gault, fifteen, had been sentenced to six years in a reformatory on the charge of making an indecent phone call. An appeal pointed out that he had not been informed of the charges against him, of his right to a lawyer, of his right to remain silent, and of his right to cross-examine his accuser.

Justice Abe Fortas, writing the majority opinion, declared, "Under our Constitution, the condition of being a boy does not justify a kangaroo court.... Neither the Fourteenth Amendment nor the Bill of Rights is for adults alone."

The Court also called the punishment harsh and unfair, pointing out that for a similar offense, like a man's using obscene language in a woman's presence, the state of Arizona imposed only a fifty-dollar fine and no more than two months in jail. The decision was reversed and the boy freed.

Nevertheless, the juvenile justice system is still easier for you to get into than out of. If you refuse to obey "reasonable and proper" orders of parents or school authorities, you can be brought to court as an "incorrigible," "ungovernable," or "unmanageable" wayward minor. When you are accused of offenses that apply only to minors, you're called a status offender because you are not accused of breaking any criminal law, only of being offensive to society because of your misbehavior. Your offenses may include truancy, running away from home, sexual misconduct, showing disrespect or refusing to obey parents or authorities, keeping "undesirable" company, fighting with siblings, disrupting classes, swearing in public, staying out late, entering bars, and being "incorrigible."

Status offenders are generally called PINS—Persons in Need of Supervision. In some states, they are known as CINS (Children in Need of Supervision), JINS (Juveniles, etc.), or just wayward minors. Some may be young people who got on the wrong side of a parent, teacher, or public official. Others may be booked as a result of police suspicion. They are mostly from poor families, because the children from white middle-class families who get into trouble are frequently not brought to court. Preferring no "scandal," their parents often send them instead to a psychiatrist, tutor, or boarding school.

Some parents, however, unable to get on the same wavelength as youngsters who defy them, sign a PINS law complaint in the hope that a juvenile court will "straighten out" their children. But that is impossible, with the case load of most judges. "A judge has about thirty minutes to deal with each offender," says Judge Joseph N. Sorrentino of the Los Angeles Municipal Court. "In that time he cannot undo fifteen years of distorted development. The juvenile court cannot be a surrogate family."

Sometimes children are just dumped into the hands of authorities by unfeeling parents. One thirteen-year-old girl was taken by her father to a police station, where he signed a PINS complaint. He left her without a word of explanation or even saying good-by.

"He never told me I was an 'incorrigible' child," she related, adding, "I didn't know I had any problems or what they were. I just knew he left me there." Bewildered, she was sent to a number of different detention centers.

About a third of the parents of runaways seek to have them incarcerated as "incorrigibles." "We don't think of incorrigibles," says Terry Moriarty of the Santa Cruz Youth Services. "We think just of families with problems who need to be taught different patterns for dealing with them."

David, almost fifteen, was brought to juvenile court as a PINS offender for staying away from home for several days at a time, even while continuing to go to school. The judge learned that he was rebelling against a year's restriction imposed by his father, preventing him from seeing any films, going with his friends on weekends, or being out past 6:00 P.M. weekdays.

The court probation officer persuaded David's father to relax this excessive discipline, imposed for a mistake the boy had made, and give David another chance. The case was then dismissed, and father and son had no further trouble.

Young people who get in trouble with the law are often those who have poor relationships with their parents. Their parents usually react in anger, rather than concern about a child's motivation, to correct what drove the child to misconduct.

"There is often a definite hostility between such children and parents," says Assistant District Attorney Robert M. Patterson, in charge of juvenile crime for Santa Cruz, California. "In court parents tell the judge, 'When we get him home, we'll guarantee he'll never do something like this again. We'll make sure he doesn't go out with those people any more.'"

PINS laws discriminate against girls. In some states, they apply to boys up to age sixteen but to girls up to eighteen. If you're a girl out late on the street, you're much more likely to be taken in by police than a boy of the same age. Almost all young people arrested for sexual misconduct are girls.

Defenders of PINS laws insist that the laws aid children by spotting early those likely to become delinquents if they are not helped. Critics believe, on the contrary, that by bringing PINS youngsters into the court system, the law makes it more likely that they *will* become delinquent. Many are confined with veteran delinquents who teach them how to "fox" authorities and get away with various kinds of street crime.

Often, too, the only rehabilitation treatment they get consists of tests and interviews, isolation for misbehavior, having to account for every five minutes of their time, denial of privacy, censorship of their mail, and deprivation of contact with the opposite sex. Such "rehabilitation" measures are not likely to improve their attitude toward society.

The public, antagonized by the amount of crime committed by youths, seldom loses sleep over what happens to delinquents or "incorrigibles." But Judge Joseph N. Sorrentino points out that only a very small percentage of young offenders are hardened criminals.

"The majority of kids are not so hopelessly embedded in the sociopath's mold," he declared. "Behind the mask of delinquency there often lives a bewildered and miserable child, emotionally starved, stunned by despair and hurting bad—a child desperately in need of one-to-one caring."

Facilities where troubled youngsters can get that kind of help are sadly lacking. Nor is there much prospect that this will change in the near future. Voters in an antitax mood are consistently refusing to fund many needed social programs.

Commissions that have studied PINS laws have generally recommended that their implementation be removed from the juvenile courts. These commissions include the President's Task Force on Juvenile Delinquency and Youth Crimes, the White House Conference on Children, the National Council on Crime and Delinquency, and a project of the American Bar Association.

A small number of states, including California and Massachusetts, have rescinded or drastically modified PINS laws. In these states, police can pick up youths for truancy, running away from home, being on the streets late at night, entering bars, and other status offenses, but they cannot lock them up. All the police can do is return them to their homes.

Arrests can be made only for the same offenses forbidden to adults. Young people can be detained, like adults, for no more than seventy-two hours, after which formal charges must be filed.

Many police in these states, angered at having their "hands tied," have refused to pick up youngsters on the loose just to return them home. As a result, runaways as young as twelve are allowed to wander around homeless, living any way they can, often resorting to theft and prostitution.

Sparky Harlan, director of San Francisco's Huckleberry House, a shelter for runaways, estimates that only five out of a hundred runaways can make it on their own.

It is difficult to describe any hard and fast rights of youthful offenders under the law because these differ from state to state. States with the best programs generally place youthful offenders on probation for a first offense. A second offense usually results in placement in a foster home or a home offering group care. The third or fourth offense could send a youngster to a camp, ranch, or farm, where he or she would be required to do hard work and a lot of exercise. These states try to avoid locking up juveniles, believing that children who are treated like prisoners are more apt to develop a prisoner mentality.

In 1974, Congress passed the Juvenile Justice and Delinquency Prevention Act, giving the states federal grants to develop small, open community facilities for PINS offenders and runaways. The states were given time to get such children out of training schools and other correctional or detention facilities.

Few states, however, have made much progress in this direction. The most desirable facilities available are those of voluntary agencies. Many reject PINS youngsters, who are often difficult slum children, as "unsuitable" for the agency programs.

In 1978, the ACLU filed a class action suit against New York voluntary agencies for discrimination. The agencies argued that they were not geared or staffed to deal with the problem. The ACLU questioned whether they were functioning to serve the needs of children or their own bureaucratic ends.

The rights of some juveniles are also sometimes ignored by police who treat them harshly. This may happen in neighborhoods with a high youth crime rate or where there is a low degree of community tolerance for teens with different life styles.

Police may also shake down youngsters they suspect of being involved in the sale and use of drugs, primarily to curb the addiction that drives victims to seek money for their habits by mugging, robbery, burglary, and larceny.

In some communities, the law simply ignores the rights of juveniles. The *Christian Science Monitor* reported the case of an Iowa boy who attended a friend's beer party while on probation. Informed, the probation officer broke into the party and took the boy into custody. He was brought to the home of a judge, who signed commitment papers in his driveway, ordering the boy immediately remanded to reform school.

Questioned about the case, the judge snapped, "The kid had a full hearing." Had the boy been an adult on probation, it is highly unlikely that he would have been jailed for the simple act of attending a beer party.

Juvenile court judges have an awesome amount of power. Cases are heard in secret, with records sealed, to protect young people from being stigmatized. But this protection also conceals possible cases of injustice by judges who may be prejudiced against female, unreligious, black, Hispanic, shaggy-haired, sullen, or defiant young defendants.

Ironically, some judges are more severe with PINS children, whose parents bring charges against them, than with delinquents, whose parents often plead for them to be freed on probation.

In the opinion of Judge David L. Bazelon of the U. S. Court of Appeals in the District of Columbia, PINS children should have the right to appeal their detention if they are not given helpful treatment in the institutions to which they are sent. They should also be able to insist upon release if they are not dangerous to themselves or others and can live in the community with the help of relatives or friends.

If you are unfortunate enough to acquire a court record because of problems in growing up, it often follows you into adulthood. You become more likely to be jailed than a person without such a record. Being called a PINS or delinquent tends to be a self-fulfilling prophecy. Youngsters often live up to their labels.

If you're seriously unhappy at home, you probably yearn to take complete control of your own life. Legally, you may leave home at the age of sixteen in most states if you can prove to a court that you are "emancipated" by being able to take care of yourself fully.

Most courts, however, require parental consent for total emancipation, which relieves parents of both their rights and responsibilities. If you're emancipated, you can live where you please, earn and keep your own money, and enjoy other adult rights.

Drinking is becoming as serious a problem among children as drugs, often spurring acts of delinquency. According to one estimate in a New York *Times* report, one in four high school students now drinks hard liquor. Children as young as eleven are being found drunk.

In many states, if you have drug or alcohol problems and are afraid to tell your parents but are desperate to be cured, you have the right to seek free treatment for addiction without the knowledge or consent of your parents.

Some parents prefer to let their teens drink, hoping it will keep them away from drugs. But most parents feel that *any* addiction—whether to liquor or to drugs—is equally dangerous to teens.

There are two ways to escape boredom, which is often the cause of addiction to liquor or drugs. Some teens do it with artificial stimulants. Others create emotional excitement for themselves by participating in dances, singing or instrumental groups, athletics, part-time jobs or volunteer work in fields of special interest, hobbies, reading, art, tinkering with cars, or other pursuits that can make the process of growing up more enjoyable.

The second way won't get you a police record.

In any court hearing or trial involving children the Constitution applies. The only difference in juvenile courts is that the proceedings are not criminal. They are usually more informal, and there is no jury.

In practice, however, constitutional rights frequently fail to protect many children who don't know they have them. Juveniles apprehended on suspicion of having committed an offense are often awed by police uniforms and the trappings of the law. Questioned, many confess. Adults who know their rights often remain silent and subsequently go free.

If you are detained by a law officer, you need answer no questions except to give your name and address. If you are taken into custody, you are entitled to at least one phone call. This is best made to parents, a close relative or friend, or a family lawyer. If you cannot afford a lawyer, the Legal Aid Society will provide one for you free.

You may not resist being searched by a police officer on the street. If you are inside your home, the officer needs a warrant. You may not resist being fingerprinted when under arrest.

To defend you properly, your lawyer needs to know the complete truth, including your reasons for anything you did. Your lawyer cannot violate your confidences. Only when your lawyer is in full possession of the facts can he or she fully protect your interests. Your lawyer may be able to show, for example, in case of a PINS detention, that your behavior was excusable because of unreasonable demands by a parent or guardian and that you are therefore not in any need of supervision. Your lawyer can also move for a dismissal of charges if any of your constitutional rights have been violated in the process of arresting and detaining you.

In most states, unless your record is a bad one, the judge will prefer to release you in the custody of your parents. Even if the offense is a serious one, some states will permit your release on bail. In others it is up to the judge.

If you are sent to a detention facility, you have the right to adequate and healthy physical conditions, proper educational facilities and opportunities, exercise periods, decent light and air, medical and psychological care as needed, freedom from overcrowding, proper clothing and bedding, laundry facilities, toilet and hygienic supplies, visitors, access to a library and reading matter, and freedom from cruel punishment.

It is no secret that many students use illegal drugs, principally marijuana. Seeking to stop the practice, some school authorities have searched school lockers. Some courts have upheld their right to do this, on grounds that the lockers belong to the schools, not the students. Other courts have authorized searches when based on reasonable suspicion, not just a whim. The ACLU recommends to school officials that school lockers not be opened without students' consent except in cases where there is a clear danger to health or safety.

The ACLU has also urged recognition of other student rights. You should not be subjected to corporal punishment. Penalties for violating regulations should be in keeping with the offense, as specified by the Eighth Amendment, forbidding "cruel and unusual punishment." Before you may be suspended or expelled, hearings should be held, after you and your parents or guardians have been notified in writing of the charges and evidence.

If you are accused, you should have the right to be represented by a person of your own choosing and be given a reasonable time to prepare your defense. You or your representatives should be allowed to examine and cross-examine witnesses and to present counterevidence. You should also have the right to remain silent at the hearing.

The school should take and provide a full record of the hearing at its expense, and you should have the right to appeal the verdict to a higher authority.

Many states prohibit discrimination against pregnant students in any way, including barring them from any classes or extracurricular activities. Other states require that if excluded, pregnant students must be provided with alternative educational facilities, such as having teachers visit in their homes.

Most school systems require attendance until age eighteen, unless you receive a high school diploma earlier. If sixteen or seventeen, you require parental consent to drop out. If you leave at sixteen, you may have to take continuing education classes until age eighteen, although school systems often don't bother about students in that category.

If you have a serious grievance against your school, you can sometimes cut through a lot of red tape and get action by an appeal to a top-ranking school district official. If your grievance seems justified, that official may take up the matter personally and be able to settle it to the satisfaction of you, your parents, and the school administrator.

A long-standing grievance of teens and parents has been the entering of unfavorable data or opinions in school records. In 1974, Congress passed a Family Educational Rights and Privacy Act. Under it, your parents are entitled to know what is in your school records, to challenge any errors, and to be informed about who will be given access to those records. If you are sixteen or older or have completed the tenth grade, you also have the right to view your own records.

In the case of juvenile records in a district attorney's office, states usually seal them after a teen-ager's eighteenth birthday. Technical print-outs of such records are then available only to police agencies or those working with them. They cannot be used in subsequent court trials, although they may be consulted by district attorneys, probation officials, police agencies, and magistrates, to judge whether leniency is warranted. Defendants with a long record of juvenile arrests do not get the benefit of the doubt; those with relatively clean records do.

Running away from home creates problems that often result in a police record of one kind or another. Janet Reed of the Children's Protective Service of Santa Cruz, California, advises young people who feel desperate about their problems not to try to solve them by flight, but to turn to a local community counseling center or youth services agency for help.

"Problem kids," she says, "take their problems with them wherever they run to."

This advice is also valid for teen-age girls who are sexually molested by their own fathers, which sometimes starts around the age of ten and continues into the teens. In the desperate hope of stopping molestation by a father, a girl may appeal to a youth service agency. She should realize that this appeal may result in the removal of the father or the girl from the home, disrupting her family life. But if a girl's mother, who invariably knows, cannot or will not stop such sexual abuse, the girl may have no other choice.

The problem is extremely serious. According to studies by Kinsey, Pomeroy, and Landis, about one in four American women have been sexually molested during childhood, whether by fathers, brothers, male relatives, or family friends. This astonishing figure was verified in an independent survey undertaken by Hank Giarretto, director of the Child Sexual Abuse Treatment Program of Santa Clara County, a federal program being tested in California.

The guilt feelings of such females may lead to self-punishing behavior. A history of forced incest has characterized the childhoods of 44 percent of female drug addicts and 75 percent of teen prostitutes.

You have the absolute right to grow up free of such molestation by any male in your family circle or outside it. By reporting it to local authorities, you will not only stop it but also bring psychiatric help to the offending male, who needs it.

YOUR RIGHTS TOMORROW

President Jimmy Carter, at a White House ceremony in 1978 announcing United States participation in the UN's Year of the Child, expressed concern over the mistreatment and neglect of millions of American children. "I don't think there is an adequate understanding yet in all our societal structure," he said, "of this devastating demonstration of carelessness or cruelty."

He noted as well that "ten million children have never received any medical care at all." There are also countless numbers who are constantly hungry. There are still people in Mississippi, for example, according to the San Francisco *Chronicle*, whose empty stomachs at bedtime keep them awake and who hear neighbors' children crying for food. Small children, given nothing for supper but a package of dried beans, scavenge in garbage cans for something to still their gnawing hunger.

The future may be a little brighter for neglected children

around the world because of the Year of the Child. The year will see $207 million in UNICEF funds spent for programs in child health, nutrition, education, social services, and emergency relief in 102 countries. It should be noted in comparison, however, that the same year will also see an expenditure of $400 *billion* by world powers on armaments.

There is a long way to go before the world's children are no longer, as sociologist Barbara Ward called them, "an endangered species."

Despite its faults and deficiencies, American society gives most of its youth more rights than young people enjoy in most other parts of the globe. Many other societies are dominated by a cult of veneration for age, which is automatically presumed to be synonymous with wisdom, while youth are regarded as too irresponsible and inexperienced to be trusted with decisions of consequence about their own lives.

But change is inevitable. TV is a powerful catalyst, presenting examples that stir youth around the world to demand more independence.

In tomorrow's world, if recommendations of the Carnegie Council on Children made in 1977 are followed, children will have more rights to make their own decisions about school curriculums; about whether to leave school to go to work; about health care; about what happens when their homes are broken by divorce, separation, or death; and about where they are placed when society sees fit to remove them from their family homes.

With regard to education, there have been various proposals for reform of high schools. Perhaps in the future the first week of the school year might be spent in individual counseling, to help every student select a program for the year. The administration and faculty could allocate their resources to the programs in demand.

Some students might be allowed to do independent study or work in volunteer services or learn as apprentices in a government office. To keep school budgets down, many students could take over much of the work that is now being done by school clerks and officials.

More relevant courses would secure and hold student interest. These may include elective seminars on racism, urban life, suburban life, drugs, human relations, foreign policy, police-youth relations, student civil liberties, the rock music culture, self-discovery, parenting, and political involvement.

Many school authorities are now considering ways of getting you more involved at various levels, from helping to plan the curriculum to the formulation of standards governing student conduct. Some state laws now permit students to petition for a student member to be included on the school district governing board for a one-year term. As students become involved in functions formerly reserved for school officials only, they are likely to manifest better feelings toward teachers and the administration, greater interest in classes, and more responsible behavior.

"Student participation in school affairs can be seen as an extension of their education," suggests the California Department of Education. "Schools should encourage students to express their opinions, to take stands on controversial issues, and to present ideas that could help improve the educational process."

Student participation in running the schools will be especially valuable to school systems by providing student feedback. School boards will be better able to determine which teachers are doing a good job of inspiring and instructing students and deserve tenure and which are deadwood that the school district would be better off without.

Tomorrow's students may not be required to complete twelve consecutive years of school or be punished as truants. Students who want or need a break before completing high school, to work or undertake some other useful experience, will in all probability be given an opportunity to return later to complete their secondary education.

Tomorrow's schools will have special diagnostic tools to help uncover any weaknesses students may have, such as problems of focusing attention, memory, finger control while writing, language, or understanding spatial relationships. Often such problems are missed by schools today, with pupils wrongly diagnosed as lazy, poorly motivated, or emotionally disturbed. "Many of these children develop behavior problems as a reaction to this humiliation," observes Dr. Melvin Levine, chief pediatrician of the Children's Hospital Medical Center, Boston. "They act out because they feel bad and need to protect themselves, rather than just sit back and fail."

Correct diagnosis of these problems in tomorrow's schools will help teachers recognize student capabilities and student handicaps. When needed, specific programs will be planned to help students overcome difficulties and experience success within their abilities.

Some social critics think that, in any case, compulsory schooling until age eighteen is unnecessary for all teen-agers and really reflects a desire by adults to keep them out of the mainstream of life for as long as possible.

Such critics believe that many teen-agers should be permitted to drop out of school to follow their own pursuits. Most educational authorities, however, consider this idea unrealistic. It ignores the fact that our increasingly complex economy requires employees with at least a high school education. But the idea of free choice for students may be one whose time has come.

We can expect to see a greater use by schools of peer counseling—group sessions for potential school dropouts led by fellow students specially trained in dealing with problems of unhappy personal relationships, drug use, family troubles, poor school attendance or study habits. Federal funds were available in 1979 for such school projects in a HOLD (Helping Overcome Learner Dropouts) program. HOLD also involves evening classes for the parents concerned.

When the young people of today become the parents of tomorrow, fathers will probably play an increasing role in the child-rearing process. When parents divorce, more and more fathers will share in the custody of the children.

The growing number of working mothers in America makes it likely that tomorrow's society will emulate the Scandinavians, Russians, and Israelis in providing widespread excellent day-care centers staffed by a mixture of fathers, mothers, older children, professional social workers, paraprofessionals, and teachers.

Because of the steady increase in the number of children born out of wedlock, as well as of child abuse cases, tomorrow's government is likely to institute compulsory high school courses for both boys and girls in child rearing.

Would-be parents may be required to obtain licenses, after proving that they have had training in parenthood. "We require licenses for driving," said one sociologist. "But millions of people unqualified to be parents are far more dangerous to the health of the nation."

In tomorrow's world, the happiest homes will continue to be those in which parents and children respect each other and have enough faith in each other's reasonableness to discuss problems calmly, to listen to each other's viewpoint thoughtfully, and then to work out compromise solutions that both can accept and live with.

It has been suggested that young people could organize, as other segments of adult society have done, to agitate for a voice in the decision-making processes of education—and, for that matter, of society and the home as well. The progress made by the women's liberation and civil rights movements during the last decade or so suggests what young people could do for themselves by organizing a children's movement.

It could, perhaps, give them a voice in Washington and in state capitals, where they now have no representation except by adults. Handicapped children testifying in legislatures and reported on by the media could have a powerful effect in obtaining legislation to permit them to function in their communities with the least restrictive kind of specialized care. School drop-outs, by explaining their reasons and indicating the changes needed in schools to keep them interested in pursuing an education, could help improve our school systems. A children's movement could also help to win recognition of each child's right to live in a world that does not contaminate its food, water, air, and soil.

Young people will probably take a much more active role in politics in tomorrow's society, as politicians are forced to reckon with the children's movement. What young people can do politically was made manifest in the 1978 election of twenty-two-year-old Stratton Taylor to the Oklahoma legislature, despite opponents' warnings not to "send a boy to do a man's job." His election was made possible by the support of children he had taught at Claremore High School. "I take this area's kids seriously," he said. "They're citizens. They know what's going on. They want to be involved."

Most child experts consider society today generally oppressive toward children, inhibiting their individuality, creativity, and self-determination.

"I have been particularly troubled by a myth . . . that we are a child-oriented society," said Professor Edward F. Zigler, former head of the U.S. Office of Child Development, "and we do all that needs to be done for our nation's children."

In his book *Birthrights*, Richard Farson urges that tomorrow's children be given "the right to exercise self-determination in decisions about eating, sleeping, playing, listening, reading, washing, and dressing. They would have the right to choose their associates, the opportunity to decide what life goals they wish to pursue, and the freedom to engage . . . in acts which are now acceptable for adults but not for children."

Tomorrow's regulatory agencies may have teen-agers appointed to serve as public watchdogs for children's interests. They could bring pressure on manufacturers who victimize children as consumers. Packages of junk foods with no nutritional value could be compelled to bear clear and honest labels, while foods hazardous to health would be outlawed. Just as liquor and cigarette advertising have been banned from TV, teen-age commissioners could help stop TV advertising that pressures children to buy and eat food that is not good for them. In January 1979, the Federal Trade Commission held hearings to consider regulations needed to control harmful advertising directed at children.

More than 7,000 small American children are injured by toys each year, despite a 1966 Child Protective Act banning hazardous toys and the false advertising of flimsy toys. Teen-agers working in regulatory agencies could compel a harder crackdown on toy manufacturers to force compliance.

In 1767, Jean Jacques Rousseau wrote in *The Social Contract*, "The most ancient of all societies, and the only one that is natural, is the family: and even so the children remain attached to the father only as long as they need him for their preservation. As soon as this need ceases, the natural bond is dissolved. The children, released from the obedience they owed to the father, and the father, released from the care he owed his children, return equally to independence."

In tomorrow's world, parents will probably set a structure of limits but give children a wide variety of choices within that structure. Having an important voice in their own affairs will help children learn how to make decisions responsibly. The limits will be steadily extended with each passing year until they blend smoothly into adult independence.

Even today, the more readily you demonstrate a willingness and ability to accept responsibilities along with privileges, the more adults will demonstrate trust and confidence in you.

The more you are accorded rights as an individual and not made to feel at the mercy of powerful adults, the more likely you are to respect adults and not make them feel like obsolete, dusty relics of a bygone era.

Adults might be reminded of these words of Abraham Lincoln: "A child is a person who is going to carry on what you have started. He is going to sit where you are sitting, and when you are gone, attend to those things which you think are important. You may adopt all the policies you please, but how they are carried out depends on him. He will assume control of your cities, states, and nations. He is going to move in and take over your churches, schools, universities, and corporations. All your books are going to be judged, praised, or condemned by him. The fate of humanity is in his hands."

Or, to bring Mr. Lincoln up to date, in *his or her* hands.

Who's running *your* life right now?

You're in good shape if your parents and teachers can answer, "We are—but less and less every year," while you reply, "I am, too—more and more each year."

Gradual emancipation means that there's a safety net under you while you try out decision-making processes.

When you've learned how to balance risks and advantages, gaining the confidence that comes with practice, you'll be ready to make it completely on your own.

BIBLIOGRAPHY AND RECOMMENDED READING

* SUGGESTED FURTHER READING

* *Academic Freedom in the Secondary Schools.* New York: American Civil Liberties Union, 1969.
Addams, Jane. *Twenty Years at Hull-House.* New York: New American Library, 1961.
Alger, Bruce. *Revolutionary Actions . . . U.S.A.* Washington, D.C.: Citizens Evaluation Institute, 1971.
Allen, Frederick Lewis. *Only Yesterday.* New York: Bantam Books, 1959.
*Archer, Jules. *You and the Law.* New York: Harcourt Brace Jovanovich, 1978.
* Aries, Philippe. *Centuries of Childhood: A Social History of Family Life.* New York: Random House, 1965.
Bagdikian, Ben H. *In the Midst of Plenty: A New Report on the Poor in America.* New York: New American Library, 1964.
* Bettelheim, Bruno. *The Children of the Dream.* New York: Avon Books, 1970.

Bleuel, Hans Peter. *Sex and Society in Nazi Germany.* Philadelphia: J. B. Lippincott Co., 1973.
Boorda, Jerry. *Access to Child Abuse Resources, Santa Cruz County 1978.* Santa Cruz, Cal.: Children's Commission, 1978.
* Bralver, Eleanor, and Lou Jacobs, Jr., eds. *Teen-agers Inside Out.* New York: Washington Square Press, 1974.
* Bremner, Robert H., ed. *Children and Youth in America.* Cambridge, Mass.: Harvard University Press, 1974.
* Burkhart, Kathryn W. *The Child and the Law.* New York: Public Affairs Committee, 1975.
Carcopino, Jerome. *Daily Life in Ancient Rome.* New Haven, Conn.: Yale University Press, 1940.
The Child in Trinidad and Tobago. Port-of-Spain: Soroptimist Club, 1970.
Chute, William J., ed. *The American Scene: 1860 to the Present.* New York: Bantam Books, 1966.
* Clopper, Edward N. *Child Labor in City Streets.* New York: Garret Press, 1970.
Coles, Robert. *The Middle Americans.* Boston and Toronto: Atlantic Monthly Press, 1971.
Committee of Concerned Asian Scholars. *China! Inside the People's Republic.* New York: Bantam Books, 1972.
Criden, Yosef, and Saadia Gelb. *The Kibbutz Experience.* New York: Schocken Books, 1976.
* De Mause, Lloyd. *The History of Childhood.* New York: Psychohistory Press, 1974.
Deuel, Wallace R. *People Under Hitler.* New York: Harcourt, Brace and Co., 1942.
* DeWar, Diana. *Orphans of the Living.* London: Hutchinson & Co., 1968.
* Dorman, Michael. *Under 21: A Young People's Guide to Legal Rights.* New York: Laurel Leaf Library, 1970.
Draper, Hal. *Berkeley: The New Student Revolt.* New York: Grove Press, 1965.
Eisenberg, Dennis. *The Re-Emergence of Fascism.* New York: A. S. Barnes and Co., 1968.
Eleven Million Teenagers: What Can Be Done about the Epidemic of Adolescent Pregnancies in the United States. New York: Alan Guttmacher Institute, 1976.

Felt, Jeremy P. *Hostages of Fortune.* Syracuse, N.Y.: Syracuse University Press, 1965.
* Fuchs, Lawrence H. *Family Matters.* New York: Random House, 1972.
Furlonge, Sir Geoffrey. *Palestine Is My Country.* New York: Praeger, 1969.
Furnas, J. C. *The Americans.* New York: G. P. Putnam's Sons, 1969.
Glazer, Nathan, and Daniel Patrick Moynihan. *Beyond the Melting Pot.* Cambridge, Mass.: M.I.T. Press, 1963.
Glock, Charles Y., Robert Wuthnow, Jane Allyn Piliavin, and Metta Spencer. *Adolescent Prejudice.* New York: Harper & Row, 1975.
* Goodman, Mary Ellen. *The Culture of Childhood: Child's-Eye View of Society and Culture.* New York: Teacher's College Press, 1970.
* Gray, George Zabriskie. *The Children's Crusade.* New York: William Morrow & Co., 1972.
Green, Timothy. *The Universal Eye: The World of Television.* New York: Stein and Day, 1972.
Halsey, Ashley, Jr., ed. *You Be the Judge.* Greenwich, Conn.: Fawcett Publications, 1961.
* Handlin, Oscar, and Mary F. Handlin. *Facing Life: Youth & the Family in American History.* Boston: Atlantic Monthly Press, 1971.
* Hartley, Shirley Foster. *Illegitimacy.* Berkeley: University of California Press, 1975.
Hill, Carol. *Subsistence U.S.A.* New York: Holt, Rinehart and Winston, 1973.
* Hoopes, Roy. *Getting with Politics: A Guide to Political Action for Young People.* New York: Laurel Leaf Library, 1968.
Hope, Marjorie. *Youth against the World.* Boston: Little, Brown and Co., 1970.
Hunter, Deirdre, and Neale Hunter, eds. *We the Chinese.* New York: Praeger, 1971.
Johnston, Mary. *Roman Life.* Chicago: Scott, Foresman and Co., 1957.
* Keniston, Kenneth, and the Carnegie Council on Children. *All*

Our Children: The American Family under Pressure. New York: Harcourt Brace Jovanovich, 1977.

Kenyatta, Jomo. *Facing Mount Kenya: The Tribal Life of the Gikuya.* London: Secker & Warburg, 1953.

* Kessen, William. *Childhood in China.* New Haven, Conn.: Yale University Press, 1975.

Keyes, Ralph. *Is There Life after High School?* New York: Warner Books, 1976.

* Law in a Free Society. *On Authority.* Santa Monica, Cal.: Law in a Free Society Project, 1972, 1973.

* ———. *On Participation.* Santa Monica, Cal.: Law in a Free Society Project, 1973.

* ———. *On Privacy.* Santa Monica, Cal.: Law in a Free Society Project, 1972.

Lens, Sidney. *Poverty: Yesterday and Today.* New York: Thomas Y. Crowell Co., 1973.

Lindner, Charles. *In the Best Interests of the Child.* New York: Federation of Protestant Welfare Agencies, 1968.

Locke, Raymond Friday, ed. *The Human Side of History.* Los Angeles: Mankind Publishing Co., 1970.

Lowenthal, David. *West Indian Societies.* New York: Oxford University Press, 1972.

Lundberg, Emma D., and Katharine F. Lenroot. *Illegitimacy as a Child Welfare Program.* Washington, D.C.: Government Printing Office, 1921.

Mandeville, Sir John. *The Travels of Sir John Mandeville.* New York: Dover Publications, 1964.

Matthews, Herbert L. *Cuba.* New York: Macmillan Co., 1966.

Milt, Harry. *The Revised Basic Handbook on Alcoholism.* Maplewood, N.J.: Scientific Aids Publications, 1977.

* Nye, F. Ivan. *School-Age Parenthood.* Pullman: Washington State University Extension Service, 1977.

Priaulx, Allan, and Sanford J. Ungar. *The Almost Revolution: France—1968.* New York: Dell Publishing Co., 1969.

Report of the Committee of Experts. Geneva: International Labour Office, 1968.

* Richette, Lisa Aversa. *The Throwaway Children.* New York: Dell Publishing Co., 1969.

Riis, Jacob A. *The Making of an American.* New York: Harper Torchbooks, 1966.

Roheim, Geza. *Children of the Desert.* New York: Harper Torchbooks, 1974.

* Sandman, Peter M. *Students and the Law.* New York: Collier Books, 1971.

Schmitt, Martin F., and Dee Brown. *The Settlers' West.* New York: Bonanza Books, 1974.

* Segal, Julius, and Herbert Yahraes. *A Child's Journey.* New York: McGraw-Hill Book Co., 1978.

Sex Education Committee. *Sex Education: A Critical Concern.* New York: New York State Coalition for Family Planning, 1975.

Shaw, Otto L. *Youth in Crisis.* New York: Hart Publishing Co., 1974.

Simone, Vera, ed. *China in Revolution.* Greenwich, Conn.: Fawcett Publications, 1968.

* Sloan, Irving J. *Youth and the Law.* Dobbs Ferry, N.Y.: Oceana Publications, 1974.

* Sorenson, Robert C. *Adolescent Sexuality in Contemporary America.* New York: World Publishing, 1973.

Spender, Stephen. *The Year of the Young Rebels.* New York: Random House, 1969.

Stallings, Captain Harold L. with David Dressler. *Juvenile Officer.* New York: Thomas Y. Crowell Co., 1954.

Stanford, Gene, ed. *Generation Rap.* New York: Laurel Leaf Library, 1971.

* *Students' Rights and Responsibilities Handbook.* Sacramento: California State Department of Education, 1978.

* Sugarman, Daniel A., and Rolaine Hochstein. *The Seventeen Guide to You and Other People.* New York: Washington Square Press, 1974.

* Sussman, Alan N. *The Rights of Young People.* New York: Avon Books, 1977.

Tannenbaum, Edward R. *The Fascist Experience.* New York: Basic Books, 1972.

Taylor, Gordon Rattray. *Rethink.* New York: E. P. Dutton & Co., 1973.

Teller, Judd L. *Strangers and Natives.* New York: Delacorte Press, 1968.

* Thorp, Roderick, and Robert Blake. *The Music of Their Laughter.* New York: Harper & Row, 1970.

* Trattner, Walter I. *Crusade For the Children.* Chicago: Quadrangle Books, 1970.
Trollope, Frances. *Domestic Manners of the Americans.* New York: Random House, 1949.
Van Buren, Abigail. *Dear Abby.* New York: Pocket Books, 1959.
Wattenberg, Ben J., and Richard M. Scammon. *This U.S.A.* New York: Pocket Books, 1967.
Wertenbaker, Thomas J. *The First Americans.* Chicago: Quadrangle Books, 1971.
Wertham, Fredric. *Seduction of the Innocent.* New York: Rinehart & Company, 1954.
Widener, Alice. *Teachers of Destruction.* Washington, D.C.: Citizens Evaluation Institute, 1971.
Wilson, Everett B. *Vanishing Americana.* New York: A. S. Barnes and Co., 1961.
Woolfolk, William, and Joanna Woolfolk. *The Great American Birth Rite: Babies as Big Business.* New York: Dial Press, 1975.
Young, Kimball. *Isn't One Wife Enough?* New York: Henry Holt and Co., 1954.
Zuckmayer, Carl. *A Part of Myself.* New York: Harcourt Brace Jovanovich, 1966.

Also consulted were issues of *American History Illustrated, Consumer Information Reports, Harvard Educational Review, IYC Newsletter, IYC Report, Mankind, Moneysworth, The Nation, Newsday, New York Civil Liberties, The New Yorker, New York Times, News of the World's Children,* San Francisco *Chronicle,* Santa Cruz *Independent,* Santa Cruz *Sentinel, School Library Journal, Teacher, The Thunderbolt, TV Guide,* and *Variety.*

In addition, brochures and reports were consulted from the American Social Health Association, British Factories Inquiry Commission, HEW Children's Bureau, International Labour Organization, Information Center on Children's Cultures, National Child Labor Committee, National Organization for Non-Parents, Public Affairs Pamphlets, Planned Parenthood Federation of America, Santa Cruz City Schools, Santa Cruz Women's Health Center, U.S. Committee for UNICEF-IYC, and Zero Population Growth.

INDEX

Abortion, 8, 113
Addams, Jane, 117
Adopted children, 15, 16–17
Affection for children, importance of, 37, 39
Agencies that can provide help to teen-agers, 67
Aiello, Stephen, 81
Alcoholism, 69
  in parents, 62
Alger, Bruce, 96
Alger, Horatio, Jr., 94
American Citizens Concerned for Life, 113
American Civil Liberties Union (ACLU), 81, 82, 87, 100, 114, 142, 146
American Journal of Orthopsychiatry, 63

American Journal of Psychiatry, 37
American Revolution, 128–129
Anderson, H. H., 48
Anker, Irving, 81
Anthony, Susan B., 73
Anton, James, 87

Baby and Child Care (Spock), 36
Bakan, David, 23
Bazelon, David L., 143
Beatles, 99
Beatniks, 86, 129
Becker, W. C., 30
Beggs, Larry, 61
Behaviorism, Watson's, 34
Berkeley student revolt, 130–131
Bilingual instruction, 50

INDEX

Birth control, 110–111, 112, 113, 115
Birthrights, 11–20
Birthrights (Farson), 154
Black children, unfair treatment of, 17–18
Blackman, Joe, 50, 52
Books, children's, 92–95
Breen, Thomas, 87
Brewer, J. E., 48
Brooks, Mel, 79
Brown, Judie, 113
Brown, Pat, 131
Brown v. *Board of Education*, 18
Brown, Wendy, 25
Bryant, Anita, 133
Burnett, Frances Hodgson, 92
Burroughs, Edgar Rice, 94
Busing, school, 18, 75

California Board of Education, 77, 81
Calvin, John, 32
Car, family, and teen-agers' rights to, 67–68
Carnegie Council on Children, 17, 150
Carter, Jimmy, 132, 149
Catcher in the Rye (Salinger), 95
Censorship
 of high school newspapers, 100–101
 of reading material, 91–92, 95–97
 of television programs and films, 97–99
Chain Saw Murders (film), 97
Child abuse, 7, 23–30, 147–148
Child and Family Counseling Center (Santa Cruz, California), 30, 97
Child and Family Services (Knoxville, Tennessee), 7
Child labor, 13, 23, 47, 117–126
Child labor laws, 122–124
Child neglect, 7, 26–27, 28, 29
Child Nutrition Act (1966), 18
Child Protective Act (1966), 154

Child's Journey, A (Segal and Yahraes), 89
Children's Bureau, U.S., 13, 15
Children's Crusade, 128
Children's movement, 153
Children's Protective Services (Santa Cruz, California), 25, 147
Children's Year (1919), 13
Cleghorn, Sarah, 121
Cleveland, Grover, 56
Clothing, choice of, and young people's rights, 85–89
Cocaine, use of, 69
Collodi, Carlo, 93
Comic books, 94–95
Communist countries, children in, 19, 35
Constitution, U.S., 9, 82, 83, 84, 132, 138, 144
Corporal punishment, 22, 45, 48, 146
Craig, James C., 74
Cytryn, L., 37

Dating, 59–60, 105, 109
Declaration of Rights of the Child (UN), 13–14
Dickens, Charles, 119
Dime novels, 93
Divorce, 39, 40, 61, 62, 105, 106, 152
Doyle, James E., 87
Dress, teen-age fashions in, 86, 87, 88
Drinking, 69, 144
Drop-outs, school, 8, 73, 77, 152, 153
Drugs, use of, 68, 69, 144, 146
Duranty, Walter, 35
Dylan, Bob, 99

Eighth Amendment, 146
Emile (Rousseau), 33
Escape from Childhood (Holt), 40
EXCEL program, 51

INDEX

Fair Labor Standards Act, 122, 123
Family, young people's rights in, 31–41, 55–70
Family Educational Rights and Privacy Act, 147
Farson, Richard, 154
Fascism of 1930s, 35
Fathers
    children's need of, 39–40
    dictatorial, 62
Federal Communications Commission, 99
Federal Trade Commission, 154
First Amendment, 82, 98, 100, 128, 132
Fletcher, Ebenezer, 129
Fortas, Abe, 138
Foster, Henry J., 27
Fourteenth Amendment, 18, 87, 138
Fourth Amendment, 81
Fuchs, Lawrence H., 47

Galea, Rev. C., 66
Gault, Gerald, 138
Gelles, Richard J., 23
Giarretto, Hank, 148
Goldberg, Mark, 4
Graham, Patrick, 30, 38, 49, 97, 99
Guelph Correctional Center, 66

Hair (musical), 87
Hair styles, teen-age, 86, 87, 88
Hale, Jacqueline, 22
Hamilton, Alexander, 118
Handicapped children, 80, 153
Hansen, Tom, 11
Harlan, Sparky, 142
Hathorne, Nathaniel, 56
Head Start, Project, 18
Henderson, Ronald W., 51
High schools, 71–84, 87, 146–147, 150
    and athletics, 78–79, 80
    curriculums of, 76–77
    early, 72–73
    grade system in, 74–75
    minority students in, 75
    newspapers for, 100–101
    and students' rights, 72, 80, 81–84, 87
    See also Public schools; Teachers
Hippies, 129–130
Hitler, Adolf, 35, 133
HOLD (Helping Overcome Learner Dropouts), 152
Holt, John, 40
Homosexuality, 68, 110
Horowitz, Roy, 23
Huckleberry House, 61, 142
Hurwitz, Craig, 4

"Illegitimate" children, 12–13, 15–16
Industrial Revolution, 118
International Labour Office (ILO), 124, 125, 126
International Year of the Child (UN), 14, 149, 150
IQ tests, 49, 50
Is There Life after High School? (Keyes), 79, 88

Jackson, Jesse, 51
Jacobson, Lenore, 49
Jacobssen, Ulla, 7
Jarvis, Howard, 134
Jaws (film), 97
Jefferson, Thomas, 5, 118
Johnson, Samuel, 97
Joplin, Janis, 79
Journal of Clinical Child Psychology, 23
"Junk" food, 27, 154
Justice under the law, young people's rights to, 135–148
Juvenile courts, 137–141, 143, 144
Juvenile delinquency, 16, 136, 137, 141, 144
Juvenile Justice and Delinquency Prevention Act, 142

INDEX

Keizer, Lewis, 77
Keniston, Kenneth, 17
Keyes, Ralph, 79, 88
Kohn, Melvin L., 41
Kojak (TV program), 98
Ku Klux Klan, 21

Legal Aid Society, 145
Legal rights of young people, 135–148
Lenin, Nikolai, 35
Lenroot, Katharine F., 15, 16
Leopold, Lynn, 4
Lesbianism, 110, 138
Levine, Melvin, 152
Ley, Robert, 35
Lincoln, Abraham, 133, 155
Livingston, Robert B., 27
Love the person of their choice, teen-agers' right to, 103–115
Lowenthal, David, 36
Lundberg, Emma O., 15

Mack, Julian, 137
Making of an American, The (Riis), 92
Malnutrition, 26–27
Mann, Horace, 44
Marijuana (pot), use of, 68, 69, 81, 146
Marriage, teen-age, 104, 105, 106
Marshall, Ray, 123
Marx, Karl, 120
May, Rollo, 38
McGuinness, Warren, 63
McKnew, D. H., Jr., 37
McNamara, Robert, 14
Mecklenburg, Marjory, 113
Menuhin, Yehudi, 35
Mercer, Jane, 50
Merriwell dime novels, 93–94
Mill, John Stuart, 46
Milt, Harry, 62
Minority groups, school problems of, 49–51
Moncharsh, Julie, 29
Moore, Kristin, 106

Moriarty, Terry, 41, 140
Mothers, working, 39
Music, teen-agers' choice of, 99–100
Mussolini, Benito, 35

National Center on Child Abuse and Neglect, 7, 24, 28
National Child Labor Committee (NCLC), 13, 121, 122
National Institute of Mental Health, 14, 41
National Institute on Drug Abuse, 69
National Runaway Hotline, 61
Nazism, 35
New Deal, 122
New York City Board of Education, 132
New York Civil Liberties Union, 81, 135
Nixon, Richard, 133

Office of Child Development, U.S., 154
Overprotection by parents, 37

Parents
 alcoholic, 62
 children's communication with, 39, 66, 115
 difficulties of, 66
 foster, 15–16
 legal responsibilities of, 68
 middle-class, 41, 46
 overprotection by, 37
 permissive, 38
 rejection by, 37
 of teen-agers, 55–70
 working-class, 41
 See also Fathers; Mothers, working
Parents Allied, 25
Patterson, Robert M., 69, 140
PCP (angel dust), use of, 68, 69
Peace Corps, 58
Permissiveness, excessive, 38
Peterson, Donald R., 39

INDEX

Pill, birth control, 110–111, 112
Pinocchio (Collodi), 93
PINS (status offenders), 139–145
Planned Parenthood, 39, 82–83, 107, 112
Pledge of Allegiance, 82, 133
Police Woman (TV program), 98
Pollution, environmental, protest against, 129, 133
Poppelreiter, Tom, 80
Portraits and Protests (Cleghorn), 121
Poverty, children born in, 17, 19, 27
Pregnancy, teen-age, out-of-wedlock, 106–108, 111, 112, 113–114
Premarital sex, 106–111, 115
Presley, Elvis, 99
Primary schools, 43–53
  See also Public schools
Privacy, pre-teens' right of, 38–39
Protection from harm, young people's rights to, 21–30
Protest against authority, young people's right to, 127–134
Psychological Care of Infant and Child (Watson), 34
Puberty, 57, 106
Public schools
  and children's rights therein, 45–53, 71–84
  early opposition to, 46, 47
  establishment of, 46
  homework assignments, 46, 74
  integration of, 18, 75
  prayer outlawed in, 82
  and scholastic ability, decline in, 51–52, 75
  See also High schools; Primary schools
Puritanism, 32–33, 44

Racism, 18
Radio, teen-age audience for, 100
Ramsey, Paul, 26
Rand Corporation, 75

Reading material, choice of and young people's rights, 91–97
Records and tapes, teen-agers' purchase of, 99, 100
Reed, Janet, 25, 147
Reed, M. F., 48
Rejected children, 37
Retarded children, 26
Right to Life Committee, National, 113
Riis, Jacob, 13, 92
Robey, A., 63
Rock-'n'-roll, 100
Rolling Stone magazine, 79
Rome, ancient, 12, 22, 44
Roosevelt, Eleanor, 133
Roosevelt, Franklin D., 122
Rosenthal, Robert, 49
Rousseau, Jean Jacques, 33, 155
Runaways, 31, 32, 61, 62, 63, 142

SACRIFICE (Student Action Committee Regarding Interests for Children's Education), 4
Salinger, J. D., 95
Saturday Night Fever (film), 115
Savio, Mario, 130
Schoenig, Terry, 4
Schools, public. *See* Public schools
Segal, Julius, 14, 89
Sex information, 96, 108, 112, 113
Sheppard-Towner Act (1921), 13
Show Me!, 96
Silent Generation, 129, 133
Simko, Robert, 4
Sit-ins, student, 3, 4
Slater, Samuel, 118
Smoking, 69
Snow, Hank, 28
Social Contract, The (Rousseau), 155
Social service and welfare organizations, 67

☞ 167 ☜

INDEX

Society for the Prevention of Cruelty to Children, 23
Sorenson, Robert C., 108, 110
Sorosky, Arthur D., 16
Sorrentino, Joseph N., 139, 141
Spargo, John, 120
Spock, Benjamin, 36
Standish, Burt L., 93
Stanford Achievement Tests, 52
Statutory rape, 108
Steele, Brandt F., 28
Stratton, Hyrum, 34
Student revolts, 130–132
Suicide, 61
Sullivan, John, 4
Supreme Court, U.S., 8, 18, 82, 83, 84, 122, 138
Synanon, 29

Taylor, Gordon Rattray, 76
Taylor, Stratton, 154
Teachers
　assaults on, 80–81
　as disciplinarians, 44, 45, 48, 49
　high school, 73, 74, 77–78, 80–81
Teen-agers
　agencies and people that can provide help for, 67
　ambivalent feelings of, 57
　dating by, 59–60, 105, 109
　and drugs, use of, 68–69
　and family car, 67, 68
　and fashions in dress and hair styles, 86–89
　"futuristic thinking" by, 64
　homosexual, 68
　and love, right to, 103–115
　moral responsibilities of, 68, 70
　parents of, 55–70
　and peer groups, 65, 88–89
　rights in the family, 55–70
　self-evaluation by, 66
　suicide by, 61
Television, 51, 97–99, 150, 154
Temme, Lloyd, 79
Tepper, Sheri, 106

Texans for America, 95–96
Third World countries, children in, 19
Tinker v. *Des Moines Community School District,* 82, 83, 132
Tomorrow, young people's rights in the world of, 149–156
Travolta, John, 115
Turner, Brian, 130
Twain, Mark, 92, 93

UNICEF, 6, 150
United Nations, 6, 13, 14, 15, 27, 149, 150

Van Buren, Abigail, 39
Venereal disease (VD), 111, 112, 113
Vietnam War, 87, 131, 132
Vitek, Jan, 125

Ward, Barbara, 150
Ward, Robert J., 96
Watson, John B., 34
Watson, W. G., 87
Wells, H. G., 120
Wertham, Fredric, 95
West Indian Society (Lowenthal), 36
White House Conference on Youth (1971), 132
Wilson, Woodrow, 13
Women's liberation movement, 80, 133, 153
Work and young people's rights, 9, 117–126

Yahraes, Herbert, 14, 89
Yankwich, Leon R., 15
Youth movements, and protest, 129–132
Youth Services (Santa Cruz, California), 41, 140

Zamora, Ronny, 98
Zigler, Edward F., 154
Zuccaro, Mary, 39, 68, 107, 110, 115